P9-DFN-673

LAS MENINAS
A Fantasia in
Two Parts

ANTONIO BUERO-VALLEJO

LAS MENINAS
A Fantasia In Two Parts

Translated By
MARION PETER HOLT

TRINITY UNIVERSITY PRESS

Trinity University Press gratefully acknowledges the assistance of the Program for Cultural Cooperation between
Spain's Ministry of Culture and United States' Universities in
making this publication possible.

Library of Congress Cataloging-in-Publication Data

Buero Vallejo, Antonio, 1916-
    [Meninas. English]
    Las Meninas : a fantasia in two parts / Antonio Buero-Vallejo ;
    translated by Marion Peter Holt.
        p.   cm.
    Translation of: Las meninas.
    Bibliography: p.xix
    ISBN 0-939980-17-7
    1. Velázquez, Diego, 1599-1660--Drama.   I. Title.
PQ6603.U4M413 1987
862'.64--dc19   87-12524
                                                                     CIP

Cover photograph: *Las Meninas,* Velázquez. Courtesy *Museo del Prado.* ©*Copyright
Museo del Prado, Madrid. All rights reserved.*

Photographs within text from the production of *Las Meninas* at Teatro Español,
Madrid, 1960. Directed by José Tamayo. Set and costumes by Emilio Burgos.
Photo credit: Gyenes.

The art beginning part two is the original music for Pavan I, included in the
SCHOTT edition of 6 PAVANS of Milán, Narciso Yepes transcription.

Printed in the United States of America

Contents

Antonio Buero-Vallejo

Introduction

Although Buero-Vallejo's first produced drama, the prizewinning *Story of a Stairway [Historia de una escalera]* in 1949, established him as the most important new playwright to appear in Spain since the Civil War, he quickly encountered the caution of commercial producers and the frustrations of censorship. *In the Burning Darkness [En la ardiente oscuridad]* was performed in 1950, followed by four other plays in a period of three years; but in 1954, *Adventure in Grayness [Aventura en lo gris]*, one of his strongest early works (begun in 1948), was denied performance, initiating a long battle with the censors.

We can only speculate on the effect the rejection of *Adventure* had on Buero's subsequent career, but it is likely that it delayed for a number of years other ventures into theatre of political implications and perhaps further experiments with the scenic device peculiar to this drama among his early plays. *Adventure in Grayness* provides with its Strindbergian dream sequence a probable first model for the nightmare scene in *The Sleep of Reason [El sueño de la razón]*, the inner mental distortions of the protagonist of *The Arrival of the Gods [La llegada de los dioses]*, and even the phantasmagorical recall of the despairing Larra in *The Detonation [La detonación]* – all works written years later.

In the first phase of Buero's career, the plays that adhered closest to conventional realism brought him the most favor with critics and audiences. Those that were more scenically inventive or metaphysically slanted had limited runs at best, and two, *The Sign We Wait For [La señal que se espera]* (1952) and *Almost a Fairy Tale [Casi un cuento de hadas]* (1953), closed in a matter of days. In 1958 Buero-Vallejo made an artistic advance that would have profound effects on the evolution of his theatre and its future impact. He abandoned the closed form characteristic of the plays of his first decade in favor of multiple stages and swift scenic transformations; he also turned to actual historical events – those surrounding the Esquilache riots of 1766 – as the subject of a play that conveyed an oblique but unmistakable political message. If not precisely a "parable" of later failures at political liberalization in Spain, *A Dreamer for a People [Un soñador para un pueblo]* did require audiences to reflect on a critical moment in Spanish history when reactionary forces prevailed over attempts at modernization.

Las Meninas was the second of Buero's plays focusing on historical figures and was staged at the Teatro Español in 1960 as part of the tricentennial commemoration of the death of Velázquez. Almost immediately Buero came under fire from traditionalists who accused him of misrepresenting Velázquez's character and of crass opportunism. The sticking point was, of course, Buero's "heretical" depiction of the painter as a man concerned with the social injustices of his time and the intimate of a confessed instigator of rebellion. The attacks, quite virulent in some instances, may well have served to guarantee the success of *Las Meninas*, for it ran for some 260 performances to become Buero's most successful production up to that time. The public response suggested more than an appreciation of a moving historical drama impressively costumed to recreate a past era. Even more forcefully than in *A Dream for a People* Buero had focused attention on contemporary conditions through recognizable historical parallels. In *Las Meninas* the challenge to the institution of state censorship was unmistakable, and Buero's Velázquez became a paradigm for the creative person whose expression is stifled by an unyielding political or artistic establishment.

Spanish critic Luis Iglesias Feijoo, writing two decades after the Madrid premiere of *Las Meninas*, is in a position to view the play far more objectively than the critics of the mid-Franco era. In his landmark study of Buero's theatre,[1] he effectively repudiates the earlier charges of misrepresentation and illustrates how Buero has transformed historical documentation, the limited biographical information that exists on Velázquez, and memoirs of the period by Jerónimo de Barrionuevo[2] into a convincing dramatic reality.

Iglesias Feijoo considers the painter a prime influence in Buero's life, "casi una figura con caracteres de mito autobiográfico" (almost a figure with aspects of autobiographical myth).[3] The seed of inspiration for the play that Buero finally wrote in 1960 had been in the playwright's mind for many years, for his fascination with the figure and art of Velázquez dates to his own first artistic efforts as a boy. In 1925, when Buero was only nine years old, he did a sketch of Velázquez's face, and the following year a similar sketch as well as a third drawing that clearly shows the painter as he appears in "Las Meninas."[4] As Iglesias Feijoo notes, Buero's first venture into writing, while still studying for his *bachillerato* in Guadalajara in 1933, was a story entitled "El único hombre" ["The Only Man"] in which the narrator enters the Prado Museum and eventually stands contemplating "Las Meninas." A year later, Buero (now an art student in Madrid) published two articles under the pseudonym "Nicolás Pertusato," the name of the young dwarf who appears in the painting and who becomes a character in the play *Las Meninas*. It would seem inevitable that once he had moved to historical themes, as he had in 1958, he would eventually undertake a dramatic work focusing on Velázquez's life and milieu.

In 1986, at the time of the revival of *The Concert at Saint Ovide [El con-*

cierto de San Ovidio], Buero stated that *The Detonation*, his drama on Larra, contained the most autobiographical allusions of any of his plays. But it is easy to detect personal links to characters or dramatic situations in other of his works, particularly *Las Meninas*. Clearly there is a personal allusion intended in Pedro's abandonment of art after his imprisonment and in the period of years (six) he spent in the galleys, which corresponds precisely to the period that Buero himself was in prison following the Spanish Civil War. More important in *Las Meninas*, however, are the lines that strongly reflect Buero's metaphysical, aesthetic, and humanitarian views. We may correctly assume that throughout the scenes between Velázquez and Pedro, in Pedro's reaction to the sketch for "Las Meninas," in Velázquez's speculations on light as the essence of the divinity, we are hearing the voice of the playwright.

Although several accounts of the career of Diego Velázquez de Silva exist, little is actually known of his private life. Unlike some other major artists, he has not been the subject of romanticized biographies, popular films, or outright fictional treatments. Since no significant writings by Velázquez have come to light, only the paintings themselves can provide suggestions as to his real nature – even though the hints they offer are sometimes as minimal as his painting technique became.

The chronicle left by his father-in-law and teacher, Pacheco, documents the painter's life up to the time of Pacheco's death in 1644, when Velázquez was forty-five. This factual biography tells us something of Velázquez's early apprenticeship, his marriage to Pacheco's daughter Juana at the age of nineteen, the birth of two daughters, and the fortuitous trip to Madrid in 1622 which led to his appointment as court painter to the young Philip IV. Later Pacheco confirms the close attachment between painter and king, mentioning that Philip frequented Velázquez's studio in the Alcázar palace to watch him paint.

Buero was criticized for his treatment of this very relationship. It was argued that no mere functionary of the court, even one who had enjoyed the king's favor and, indeed, friendship for three decades, would dare address the monarch as Velázquez does in the play. But this assumption is based on general knowledge of *normal* social deportment in the period between individuals of different stations. We may well wonder if an exceptional man like Velázquez might not have risked breaking the rules in matters other than art. Buero is by no means alone in seeing more than a distant, formal association between the king and a court painter whose official appointments put him in increasing proximity to the royal personage. In his biography of Velázquez, art critic-historian Jonathan Brown indicates that there is good reason to believe that by 1650 (more than 25

years after the painter's original appointment to the court) the relationship between Velázquez and Philip IV "had evolved into something like a
friendship. . . ."[5] Undisputed is the fact that Velázquez defied the king during his intriguing second trip to Italy (1649-51) by staying abroad longer
than Philip wished.

A re-creation of Velázquez's relationship with his wife can only be
based on conjecture, but it is not unreasonable to speculate on the nature
of a union that was barren except for its first three years. Buero in no way
sensationalizes Velázquez's domestic situation, but he does create a credi-
ble conflict between an emotionally neglected wife and a husband whose
art and official duties took precedence. It is this very conflict that leads to
the accusations raised against the painter in part 2 of *Las Meninas*. Buero's
Velázquez, by his uniqueness as an artistic visionary, seems destined to
be misunderstood and the victim of jealousy not only from those who
lack his talent but also from those closest to him: Juana and his apprentice
Juan de Pareja.

In seventeenth-century Spain, painters were considered craftsmen,
their social position no different from that of other artisans. Velázquez's
known aspirations for higher recognition have often been cited as a domi-
nant influence in his adult life. While Buero in no way denies such ambitions for courtly honors, intimated early in the play by mention of the

Luis Rico Sáez as Nicolasillo and Lina de Hebia as Mari Bárbola, Teatro Español,
Madrid, 1960. *Photo Credit: Gyenes.*

Cross of Santiago, he depicts Velázquez as a man whose art overshadows all other considerations and as the humanitarian many of his paintings suggest to the contemporary viewer. Time and again there are tantalizing hints of the painter's concern for his models, though no firm evidence confirms a capacity for the friendship Buero's Velázquez enjoys for a brief but decisive period with the aged rebel Pedro.

Pacheco describes his pupil's interest in painting "bodegones" or inn scenes depicting ordinary people in daily situations, and later Velázquez would paint the dwarfs of the court with the same brilliance as he painted the royalty he served and who provided his sustenance. José Gudiol, in his biographical study, views the paintings of the deformed as forerunners of Goya's depictions of the harshest aspects of life and asserts that although Velázquez never went as far as Goya in his choice of subject, "he shows the feeling of protest that Goya, in very different ways, was to make one of the principal signs of his art."[6] Gudiol particularly stresses the elements of humanism in Velázquez's art and the absence of any trace of irony or ridicule in his treatment of deformed and socially marginal subjects. This opinion, written by an art critic and historian more than a decade after the premiere of *Las Meninas*, essentially sustains Buero's theatrical portrayal of Velázquez as an individual of deep compassion.

Buero's plays frequently draw upon and refer to actual works of art, even beyond the specific scenes where a painting or etching is turned into a dramatic action developing from an onstage replication of the work ("Las Meninas," Goya's etching "El sueño de la razón produce monstruos," and the eighteenth-century etching of blind musicians in *The Concert at Saint Ovide*).[7] Velázquez's painting "Fable of Arachne" (also known as "The Spinners") becomes the focal point of *Secret Dialogue [Diálogo secreto]* (1984). Here the audience watches the painting fade into black and white, losing coloration, as it is led through one of Buero's most startling scenic transformations into the troubled thoughts of a color-blind art critic. In some instances a painting complements historical documentation in character delineation and, to be sure, in defining costume, makeup, and overall physical appearance. In *A Dreamer for a People*, a replica of Mengs's portrait of the Marqués de Esquilache hangs prominently in the room where the character will first appear in the play. *The Sleep of Reason* offers not only the example of Leocadia (drawn from the Black Painting that is sometimes called "La Leocadia") but also careful theatrical re-creations of Ferdinand VII, Dr. Arrieta (with Goya himself), and Father Duaso – all subjects of paintings by Goya.

Although no painting by Velázquez is actually seen in a performance of *Las Meninas* (at least not in Buero's original scenic concept), the painter's

Las Meninas, Teatro Español, Madrid, 1960. Set and costumes by Emilio Burgos. Directed by José Tamayo. *Photo Credit: Gyenes*

art is omnipresent in the characters themselves. Of the eleven humans who are immortalized in the painting "Las Meninas," nine appear as actual characters in the play. Only Queen Mariana (her portrait with the king reflected in a mirror) and the little Infanta Margarita do not figure in the action preceding the final tableau. Three other historical characters — Mazo, Pareja, and María Teresa — are also subjects of paintings by Velázquez, while Martín and Pedro are fictional creations based on the anonymous models who posed for "Aesop" and "Menippus." These totally invented but art-inspired characters are perhaps the most provocative in *Las Meninas,* for they relate to the dramatic action in ways unprecedented in Buero's theatre. Pedro, based on the painting representing the sixth-century Greek fabulist, serves multiple functions: he is both Velázquez's conscience and the complement the painter seeks but has not found in his family or the court. He also represents the voice of the people and, slightly transformed, will reappear in a similar role (and by the same name) in Buero's later historical play *The Detonation* (1977). Martín, who reflects the cynicism attributed to the classical Menippus both in Velázquez's painting and in his theatrical incarnation, is the first of Buero's characters to speak directly to the audience outside the frame of dramatic action. Such a commentator may easily be viewed as a Brecht-inspired device to distance the audience from the ensuing interpretation of historical events, but Martín may actually encourage a subtle form of audience participation. Iglesias Feijoo convincingly defends his contention that Martín, "full of calculated ambiguity," is not particularly Brechtian.[8] Although it would appear that he is speaking to the audience in the opening scene, he immediately asserts that his words are directed to the pavement stones or the air; he then turns to the audience and treats it as if it were an assembly from his own time (the seventeenth century), initiating a process of fictionalization of the audience itself, inviting its participation as a silent character belonging to the world of fiction.

Las Meninas is one of Buero-Vallejo's most eloquent plays, and its dialogue provides special insight into his views about the creative process, the function of art, and the dilemma of the visionary creator – artist, writer, musician, political mover – in an authoritarian or reactionary society. Like *The Sleep of Reason*, his later and better known drama on Goya, *Las Meninas* also transcends both the historical moment of its action and the conditions that prevailed in Spain at the time of its first production.

Las Meninas was completed in October 1960, some ten years before *The Sleep of Reason* reached the stage. For all the thematic parallels that might be drawn between the two, scenically their differences are considerable. The earlier play is intentionally suggestive and evocative, reflecting the

Victoria Rodríguez, Carlos Lemos, and Javier Loyola.*Las Meninas,* Part II, Teatro Español, Madrid, 1960. *Photo Credit: Gyenes*

painterly techniques of Velázquez himself, while the later work literally assaults the audience's perceptions with projections of Goya's disturbing and even shocking "Black Paintings." The American critic Robert Nicholas was the first to observe the correlation between Buero's dramatic techniques in part 1 of *Las Meninas* and Velázquez's impressionism:

> Many things are suggested but none explained or justified. Attention moves quickly from one character to another, from one place on stage to another. The result is an enigmatic kaleidoscope of purposeful confusion and suspicion... Life is seen as snatches of overheard remarks and signs just as colors can be seen as snatches of hues and tones in an impressionistic painting.[9]

The two plays also differ notably in their spatial conceptions. *Las Meninas* offers a panoramic view of events in which private encounters are set apart and allows for the interaction of the intimate scenes within a larger frame of action. *The Sleep of Reason* is intensely claustrophobic, representing Goya's sensorial isolation as well as his virtual imprisonment in his country estate after the restoration of the tyrannical Fernando VII. In this respect it resembles the later *The Foundation [La fundación]* (1974), which is perhaps Buero's definitive expression of claustrophobia. The panoramic theatricalization of history was not, however, a passing phase in Buero's theatre; when we look forward to *The Detonation* of 1977, we find another intimate personal drama (that of the suicidal Mariano José de Larra) played out within a larger frame of social, cultural, and political events.

In keeping with his practice of avoiding conventional theatrical labeling, Buero calls *Las Meninas* a "fantasía velazqueña" rather than a "drama," and it is well to keep in mind that "fantasía" means both "fantasy" and, in music, "variations on a theme at the will of the composer."[10] Not only does the musical connotation of the descriptive title suggest Buero's approach to interpreting and elaborating on events of Velázquez's life – or, more specifically, to this thematic use of the painting "Las Meninas" – it also alerts us to actual allusions to musical form in the play. Indeed, the first act ends with overlapping verbal exchanges that parallel in dialogic terms such familiar operatic passages as the quartettes in Verdi's *Rigoletto* and Puccini's *La Boheme*, where two separate sung conversations are woven together to provide striking dramatic contrasts. The final tableau of *Las Meninas* is less overtly operatic but no less suggestive of operatic possibilities (and perhaps inspiration) as an ensemble piece which introduces and blends a variety of conflicting thoughts unified through harmonic development of a single theme.

Buero-Vallejo's plays from the moment of his first success with *Story of a Stairway* in 1949 were characterized by experimentation in form and the introduction of visual or aural elements designed to achieve a degree of participation from audiences all too accustomed to the passive theatrical experience. Sometimes these were paraverbal signals that underlined a dramatic situation or eliminated the need for an actual verbal explanation. The accidental kicking over of the milk pitcher by two lovers destined to separate in *Story of a Stairway* or the overturning of the chess figures near the end of *In the Burning Darkness* are merely symbolic prefigurations (undoubtedly reflecting Buero's particular admiration for Ibsen). But in the "test" scene of the latter work, a blind young man, in a moment of sudden realization, avoids a table placed in his path to trip him, transmuting the visual into a major instrument of dramatic expression.

The scenic devices most typical of Buero's theatre have been abrupt visual or aural transformations which draw the spectator into an actual physical experience analogous to that of a character on stage. These have included absolute darkness (for blindness), absolute silence (for deafness), colors fading to black and white (for colorblindness), and onstage depictions of the illusion (or delusion) of a character that are shared by the audience but not by other characters in the play. These devices were first called "efectos de inmersión" or "immersion-effects" by the Spanish critic Ricardo Doménech;[11] however, Buero himself had already referred to the procedure by the more encompassing term "interiorización" (interiorization). The pure or total immersion-effects invariably involve an actual *physical* experience on the part of the spectator if in performance the effect is properly achieved in a technical sense. Other effects, which are generally ancillary to the moment, trigger a thematic, metafictional, or identity association that intensifies the dramatic experience, preventing the spectator from merely viewing an action performed within a frame. These secondary effects tend to stimulate the audience psychologically rather than physically.

Las Meninas has no "total" immersion-effects comparable to the absolute darkness of the murder scene in *The Concert of Saint Ovide*, which was written two years later, or the recurring silences of *The Sleep of Reason*. There are, however, two notable moments of interiorization in the play and, in the final scene, a memorable reconciliation of interiorization and Brechtian distancing. The first two immersion scenes both involve the viewing by characters of a painting or sketch that the audience does not see (which are, incidentally, works by Velázquez that are no longer in existence).[12] In part 1, Velázquez allows Mazo and Pareja to view a nude that he keeps concealed because of prohibitions dictated by the Inquisition. As they react onstage to what is out of sight of the audience, Milán's

"Second Pavan" (played on a vihuela) is heard from offstage, in effect suggesting the unseen painting synesthetically. The second and more hyp-
notic instance of immersion occurs near the end of the act when the
nearly blind Pedro Briones "sees" the sketch for the painting that will
eventually be known as "Las Meninas." The accompanying musical motif,
the "Fantasia" by Fuenllana,[13] is heard again to initiate the final tableau
representing the painting, and here it confirms its intended thematic association. The music continues as Martín (functioning now as "stage director") animates the figures momentarily and increases in volume as the
stage lights fade.

Buero's use of musical motifs dates to his first play, *In the Burning Darkness* (written in 1946), in which Beethoven's "Moonlight Sonata" provides a
background for a conversation between two blind young women. Later in
the same play, "Aase's Death," from Grieg's incidental music for *Peer Gynt*,
accompanies an offstage murder as the violent act is watched from onstage
by a character helpless to intercede. Buero may well have made these
musical selections instinctively, and their potential metafictional allusions
may be a by-product of which he was not fully aware at the time. Although
he employed music or sound motifs in several other plays of his first decade, it is only in his second phase that specific musical phrases become sig-
natures for characters or function in a wider semiotic sense as co-equals
with other verbal or aural aspects of his plays. The more subtle use of the
musical motif begins with *The Foundation*, and all of Buero's subsequent
plays contain themes with a metafictional or thematic function considera-
bly more intricate than we find in *Las Meninas*. Yet when we compare the
function of the "spring concerto" from Vivaldi's "Le quattro stagione," which
simply begins and ends *A Dreamer for a People*, and the use of compositions
by Milán and Fuenllana as individual motifs in *Las Meninas*, it becomes
apparent that Buero's concept of the integral role of music in his plays was
already becoming more specific.[14]

Of Buero's four plays dealing with aspects of Spain's past, only *The Sleep
of Reason* has enjoyed extensive production since its original staging. The
reasons are not difficult to determine and are unrelated to the intrinsic
dramatic power of the other three works. *A Dreamer for a People, Las
Meninas*, and *The Detonation* not only require large scenic spaces to
accommodate their panoramic features but also demand period costum-
ing for casts that number 25, 24, and 44 respectively – numbers that are
intimidating even when allowing for some reduction through the dou-
bling of actors in multiple roles.[15] The relative obscurity outside Spain of
their respective focal characters, the Marqués de Esquilache and Mariano
José de Larra, has created an additional obstacle to production of *A*

Dreamer for a People and *The Detonation;* but *Las Meninas,* dealing in compelling dramatic terms with an artist and a painting of almost universal recognition, would seem a likely candidate for reevaluation and imaginative staging. In light of Buero's subsequent use of projections in *The Sleep of Reason* and musical or sound motifs in a variety of plays, it is possible to imagine a multimedia approach to the work in which projections of Velázquez's paintings and more extensive motifs underscore a less literal staging than specified in Buero's original concept for the Italianate Teatro Español. Directors must be mindful, however, of essential differences between *Las Meninas* and *The Sleep of Reason.* A pervasive impressionism informs both dialogue and scenic effect, and the dramatic conflict leads to a final moment of temporal suspension in which the audience is invited to embark on the "ship" of Velázquez's studio. These elements exclude the type of visual-aural assault that is so integral a part of the scenic realization of the later play. Perhaps any consideration of Buero's two dramas on artists and their historical milieu should begin with a contemplation of the individual works that give them their titles: the painting "Las Meninas" and the etching "The Sleep of Reason Produces Monsters." Director, scenic and lighting designer, actor – and critic – will find a guide to the playwright's intent in the sources of his own inspiration.

NOTES

1 Luis Iglesias Feijoo, *La trayectoria dramática de Antonio Buero Vallejo* (Santiago de Compostela: Universidad de Santiago de Compostela, 1982), pp. 265-77.

2 Jerónimo de Barrionuevo's *Avisos,* dealing with the years 1654-58, provided Buero with background material that he wove with great effectiveness into the play. This includes references to rumors about the treasure buried in Balchín del Hoyo, a ball of fire seen in the sky, and reports of the uprisings in Lorca, La Rioja, and other locations. Buero also drew from Antonio Palomino's *El museo pictórico y escala óptica* (Madrid, 1715-24) material that lends authenticity to the play. An English translation of Palomino's work is included in Enriqueta Harris' *Velázquez,* Oxford, 1982.

3 Iglesias Feijoo, 261.

4 These early drawings are reproduced in "Regreso a Buero Vallejo," *Cuadernos 13, El público* (April 1986):10-11.

5 Jonathan Brown, *Velázquez, Painter and Courtier* (New Haven and London: Yale University Press, 1986), p. 240. Brown's acclaimed biography is generally considered definitive and can be recommended as the best source in English on Velázquez.

6 José Gudiol, *The Complete Paintings of Velázquez*, trans. Kenneth Lyons (1974; New York: The Viking Press; New York: Greenwich House, 1983), p. 207.

7 The only comparable use of art in American theatre has been the Stephen Sondheim-James Lapine musical *Sunday in the Park with George*, in which the figures in a painting by Georges Seurat are re-created as characters on stage.

8 Iglesias Feijoo, pp. 279-80.

9 Robert L. Nicholas, *The Tragic Stages of Antonio Buero Vallejo* (Chapel Hill: Ediciones de Hispanófila, 1972), pp. 66-67.

10 Definition from *The American Heritage Dictionary of the English Language* (1973).

11 Ricardo Doménech, *El teatro de Buero Vallejo* (Madrid: Editorial Gredos, 1973), pp. 49-52.

12 The nude painting that Mazo and Pareja view is not the familiar "Rokeby Venus" (or "Nude with a Mirror") now in London's National Gallery, but one of the three other nudes known to have been painted by Velázquez and which are now lost. The sketch of "Las Meninas" that Velázquez later shows to Pedro is one we may assume the painter made prior to painting the actual canvas.

13 Luys de Milán (b. 1500?-d. 1561?) was a composer and courtier who, like Velázquez, traveled to Italy and was influenced by Italian culture. Miguel de Fuenllana (d. 1579) was born near Madrid, probably during the first or second decade of the sixteenth century. It is hardly a coincidence that Buero chose a theme by this composer, who was blind from infancy, to illustrate beauty as seen by the nearly blind Pedro.

14 It is significant that in the first published version of *Aventura en lo gris (Teatro*, 10, 1954) the stage directions at the beginning of the dream sequence specify "una música lenta y sorda" (a slow, muffled music). In editions of the play published since the premiere of the revised version in 1963, the description becomes: "Muy remota, la música de 'Sirenas' de Debussy . . ." (Far-off, the music of Debussy's "Sirènes" . . .).

15 *Las Meninas* was televised in Czech in 1967 in a version by Vladimir Oleriny (Bratislava TV, Czechoslovakia).

Selected Readings on Buero-Vallejo and Las Meninas

The following list of readings in three languages is drawn from the extensive and growing bibliography on the theatre and life of Antonio Buero-Vallejo. Selections are limited to book-length studies which deal with *Las Meninas* in more than a cursory or purely descriptive manner and to articles touching on some essential aspect of this play.

In English

Dixon, Victor. " 'The immersion-effect' in the Plays of Antonio Buero Vallejo." *Drama and Mimesis, Themes in Drama 2.* Ed. James Redmond. Cambridge: Cambridge University Press, 1980, 113-37.

Edwards, Gwynne. *Dramatists in Perspective: Spanish Theatre in the Twentieth Century.* New York: St. Martin's Press, 1985.

Halsey, Martha T. "Esquilache, Velázquez and Quevedo: Three Historical Figures in Contemporary Spanish Drama," *Kentucky Romance Quarterly,* 17.2 (1970), 109-126.

_____. *Antonio Buero Vallejo.* New York: Twayne, 1973.

Molina, Ida. "Authority versus Truth in *Las Meninas* and in *Galileo,*" *Hispanófila,* 57 (1976), 61-64.

Nicholas, Robert. *The Tragic Stages of Antonio Buero Vallejo.* Chapel Hill: Estudios de Hispanófila, 1972.

O'Connor, Patricia W. "Censorship in the Contemporary Spanish Theatre," *Hispania* 52.2 (1969), 282-88.

Perri, Dennis. *"Las Meninas*: The Artist in Search of a Spectator," *Estreno* 11.1 (1985), 25-29.

Ruple, Joelyn. *Antonio Buero Vallejo: The First Fifteen Years.* New York: Eliseo Torres and Sons, 1971.

In Spanish

Doménech, Ricardo. *El teatro de Buero Vallejo.* Madrid: Gredos, 1973.

Iglesias Feijoo, Luis. *La trayectoria dramática de Antonio Buero Vallejo.* Santiago de Compostela: Universidad de Santiago de Compostela, 1982.

Paco, Mariano de, ed. *Estudios sobre Buero Vallejo*. Murcia: Universidad de Murcia, 1984.
[*This volume contains an introduction and twenty-five reviews, sketches, and critical studies in Spanish or English written between 1949 and 1984. Reprinted are the articles by Dixon and O'Connor listed above.*]

Pérez-Stansfield, María Pilar. *Direcciones de teatro español de posguerra*. Madrid: José Porrúa Turanzas, 1983.

In Italian

Ruggeri Marchetti, Magda. *Il teatro di Antonio Buero Vallejo o il processo verso la veritá*. Rome: Bulzoni, 1981.

Translator's Note

Translators of stage scripts must be mindful of the prime purpose of their words: to serve as a basis for a theatrical presentation of the play by a director, actors, and technicians before an audience who will react to what they see and hear. If translators and their collaborators in the theatre work their transformations with art, the audience will never be distracted by the thought that the script existed first in another language. This prime function of a play – whether from ancient Greece or modern Europe – does not change even though playwrights may become literary figures and their words the subject of analysis and study. With this English version of *Las Meninas*, as with my earlier translations of Buero-Vallejo's plays, my aim has been playability, while attempting to re-create the essential tone and verbal suggestions of the original.

By selective use of forms of address and words associated with the seventeenth century, Buero suggests the time of the play's action without lapsing into the artificiality that sometimes threatens the verisimilitude of historical drama. At the same time, he scrupulously avoids anachronisms or contemporary colloquialisms that would negate the sense of period. Even though the court rituals place certain limitations on the degree of intimacy between characters of different stations (as in the private scene between Velázquez and María Teresa), the dialogue remains subtle, with abundant innuendo where directness is impossible. When characters do shed their verbal masks, or add a note of scorn or irony to the formalities (as does the beggar Martín), the theatrical effect is all the more compelling. The most memorable and revealing scenes of the play are, I believe, those between Velázquez and Pedro. When the half-blind Pedro "views" the sketch for "Las Meninas," the dialogue reaches a level of eloquence matched in Buero's theatre only by Goya's speech to Arrieta (in *The Sleep of Reason*) on art in a repressive society.

The translator of Buero-Vallejo's *Las Meninas* must also be constantly aware of Velázquez's "Las Meninas," which is the central theme on which this "fantasia" is developed. The painting suggests, apart from Buero's dramatic use of it, a theatrical experience – a participatory experience that provokes an emotional as well as an intellectual reaction in the viewer. Both the content of the play and statements by Buero in his essay "El espejo de 'Las Meninas' " (in *Tres maestros ante el público*, Madrid, 1973) confirm the playwright's keen awareness of the wider implications of Velázquez's masterpiece and the suggestive powers of its remarkable grouping of eleven humans (two of them seen only as painted images reflected in a mirror) and a dozing animal. Since the Spanish title of the painting has acquired virtually universal recognition and signifies today far more than the two figures on the canvas who actually qualify as "meninas" or "ladies in waiting," I have retained the original Spanish title for the English version.

With the publication of *Las Meninas* (his thirteenth full-length work) in 1961, Buero initiated a practice he has continued with all the Spanish editions of his plays to the present. Cuts and modifications made in the script during the production of each play are restored in brackets in the printed text. Buero wrote that his purpose was to protest the custom in Madrid of nightly double performances (at 7:00 and 10:45) that limited the playing time to a little over two hours at most – in effect creating a kind of economic restraint on creativity. He also noted, however, that he was not suggesting that the restored cuts improved the play – though he was arguing for his own right to develop a dramatic situation at a more leisurely pace than the entrenched performance system permitted. (The double performance still prevails in commercial houses in Spain, but the single evening performance is increasingly common in the subsidized national and municipal theatres). As with my translations of *The Sleep of Reason* and *The Foundation*, I have made selective use of the production cuts, restoring those that contribute to an effective English rendering but observing others that are in some sense reiterative. None of the cuts in *Las Meninas* occurs in the critical scenes between Velázquez and Pedro, and none involves the omission of a scene or episode. The single brief cut that eliminated a purely visual moment (in part 2) has been restored. These modifications should not be confused with censorship deletions. The ten or so cuts, ranging from a single line to a paragraph, originally requested by the censors in 1960, were all salvaged and eventually restored without substantive changes through the efforts of director José Tamayo.

Although Buero's notations in *Las Meninas* for lighting, sound, and other stage effects are somewhat less involved than those in many of his plays, they remain an inseparable part of his dramatic concept. In order to simplify Buero's initial set description, I have removed the detailed specifications for Velázquez's studio and placed them at the end of the play where the set designer may determine the precise dimensions and contents of this scenic space fundamental to any staging of the play.

I thank Susana Powell of the Ph.D. Program in Theatre at the CUNY Graduate Center for her careful reading of my original translation script and Lois A. Boyd, director of Trinity University Press, for invaluable editorial counsel.

M.P.H.

LAS MENINAS
Part One

Characters (in order of appearance)

MARTÍN
PEDRO BRIONES
A DOMINICAN FRIAR
MARÍA AGUSTINA SARMIENTO
ISABEL DE VELASCO
MARCELA DE ULLOA
DIEGO RUIZ DE AZCONA
A BURGUNDIAN GUARD
JUANA PACHECO [WIFE OF VELÁZQUEZ]
JUAN BAUTISTA DEL MAZO
JUAN DE PAREJA
DIEGO VELÁZQUEZ
INFANTA MARÍA TERESA
JOSÉ NIETO VELÁZQUEZ
ANGELO NARDI
THE MARQUÉS
NICOLASILLO PERTUSATO
MARI BÁRBOLA
KING PHILIP IV
A COURT USHER
A COURT OFFICIAL
FIRST CONSTABLE
SECOND CONSTABLE
INFANTA MARGARITA

[Madrid, during the autumn of 1656]

The Set

At the time of the action, Velázquez lived in the "Casa de Tesoro" or "Treasury House," an annex to the east of the old Royal Palace in Madrid. It is assumed that he could have glimpsed the windows and balconies of the royal apartments from his own house. A central playing area, raked and elevated two steps from stage level, alternately represents Velázquez's studio or workroom in the palace, as depicted in the painting "Las Meninas," and the interior of his house. A simple curtain can be used to effect the scene change by closing off the upstage section; a second curtain, further downstage, can close off the entire central area at the times indicated in the play, or lighting changes may be substituted. An armchair and a smaller chair placed downstage a bit left of center will serve for scenes in both the palace and Velázquez's house.

The central area is flanked by two façades which are slightly angled toward each other. The right façade, representing the exterior of the Treasury House, has a main door at street level and a balcony with an iron railing above it. The opposite façade, representing the exterior of the palace, has a large grilled window on the lower level and an imposing balcony reached through double doors above. Although both are of the same architectural style, they should not be symmetrical. The one at left is a bit higher and wider to suggest its greater importance. Slate-roofed spires crown both façades. In front, an apron runs the full width of the stage to represent the palace courtyard and to provide additional playing areas. In the background, a drop or projection shows more of the palace; above it all, the vivid blue sky of Madrid.

For a thrust or arena stage, variations are possible as long as care is taken to preserve the basic spatial relationships essential to the performance of the overlapping scenes and moments of overlapping dialogue.

[A detailed description of the dimensions and decoration of Velázquez's studio is provided at the end of the play.]

José Bruguera as Martín, posed as the model for "Menippus," Teatro Español, Madrid, 1960. *Photo Credit: Gyenes.*

José Sepúlveda as Pedro, posed as the model for "Aesop," Teatro Español, Madrid, 1960. *Photo Credit: Gyenes.*

PART ONE

The distant tolling of a bell ceases shortly after the lights come up. The stage is in dark shadows. Two strongly spotted figures stand motionless downstage on opposite sides. They are the two beggars who, some sixteen years before, served as models for Velázquez's ironic versions of Menippus and Aesop. The resemblance is complete, but time has had its effects on both men. Martín — the name given in the play to the rogue who lent his face and form to Menippus — now has much grayer hair. Muffled in his frayed cloak and wearing a grimy hat, he maintains at stage right the pose in which he was painted. Stage left, Pedro — who was painted as Aesop — does the same. Although his loose tunic is not the same one in the painting and may even be a different color, it recalls unmistakably the one he wore when his likeness was captured. He is not carrying the book under his right arm now, but in its place he is holding a coil of rope. Already old when he met Velázquez, he is now approaching eighty, with totally white hair. But his strong repelling face has hardly changed. Overcome by age and almost blind, he has found something to lean against while he waits for his companion to help him.

MARTÍN [*To the audience*]   No, we're not paintings. We spit, we speak, or we keep our mouths shut, depending on how the wind is blowing. And we're still alive. [*He looks toward Pedro.*]   Well, me more than him. He's on his last legs, and there's not much I can do about it. The painter from Seville caught us just as we were, and we may have changed a little. But as you know, some things stay with us to the grave.

PEDRO   Who are you talking to, madman?

MARTÍN [*Laughs. Confiding*]   He's almost blind but he knows I'm not speaking to anybody. What if I do talk to the stones in the street? He's done some crazier things than that in his time. You'll see what I mean.

PEDRO   Enough is enough!

MARTÍN [*Winks. He takes a few short steps and gestures like a carnival mountebank, speaking for the benefit of imaginary onlookers who are not the audience for the play.*]   Talking to the air is a way of surviving. You tell things as they might have happened and that makes it all easier to bear. [*To the real audience*]   So I'll return to you and I'll continue: In that year of our Lord 1656, the bells of the church of San Juan were tolling when my friend and I reached the house of

Don Diego Velázquez, the painter from Seville.

[*The lights come up. It is a bright day. Curtains conceal the central playing area.*]

You don't know that story?   [*He laughs.*]   I make up a lot of tales, but this one could be true. Who says it's not? You, sir?...You, milady?...You keep your mouths shut, don't you? No opinions. [*He looks right and lowers his voice.*]   I keep mine shut too.   [*He puts a finger to his lips.*]   Shhhh!

[*A Dominican Friar enters right and crosses. Martín approaches him with a great show of obeisance while Pedro tries to make out what is happening.*]

May our Lord grant the most reverend father a long life.

[*The Dominican offers him his rosary. Martín kisses it as the Friar blesses him. After a quick glance at Pedro, who has not moved, the Friar exits left. Martín turns to the audience.*]

If a man gives you his blessing, you shouldn't ask for money. He's a Dominican; he could belong to the Holy Tribunal, and you know it's best to stay clear of the Inquisition. That's why I stopped my story when I saw him coming. As I said, I brought my old friend to the house of Velázquez. We had got to know each other well when he painted us, pretending that we were two ancient philosophers. I remember asking him then: Don Diego, were those philosophers poor too? And he told me yes. And I said: but their rags weren't like ours, were they? And he answered: rags always look the same. He laughed at that and my friend laughed too. I couldn't tell you why, but they understood each other. Afterwards, my friend left Madrid and I didn't see him for many years. We've been together again for three months now, and things haven't gone too bad for us. We've earned enough for food, carrying bundles or rich people around in their sedan chairs. But he's getting too old for that, and he's been having chills a lot. Now he's got it into his head that he has to see the painter from Seville.

[*He stops when he sees Pedro making his way to the steps and sitting down.*]

What's the matter?

PEDRO   Just tired.   [*Martín sits beside him.*]

MARTÍN   [*Sadly*]   So am I.

PEDRO   You can go about your business. I know where I am.

MARTÍN   I've got time. Listen, why is it so important for you to see him? You're not just looking for a good meal. I know you better than that.

PEDRO   That's my concern.

MARTÍN   You don't even know if he'll let you in.

PEDRO   [*Giving him a violent shove*]   Just leave me alone!

MARTÍN   Maybe he shouldn't let you in. When you came here from Rioja three months ago, you'd grown a beard. And you'd found yourself a new name – not the one I knew you by sixteen years ago. And you shaved regularly in those days. The palace air might not be so healthy for you.

PEDRO   Shut up!   [*He gets up and takes a few steps right. Martín follows and takes him by the arm.*]

MARTÍN   Wait . . . Look up there. Those are the rooms of the Infanta. Can you see? There's someone at the window. Maybe the dwarfs are coming out . . .

[*It's not the dwarfs who appear but two of the Meninas, or Ladies-in-Waiting, of the little Infanta.*]

No, it's just the girls who watch over the Infanta. They've tossed me a few coins. Maybe another one will tinkle down.   [*He leaves Pedro, who gives him a disdainful look, and goes toward the balcony. Doña María Agustina Sarmiento and Doña Isabel de Velasco have opened the windows and step out cautiously. They are quite young: Agustina perhaps no more than sixteen and Isabel nineteen. They are wearing the same dresses as in the painting "Las Meninas."*]

AGUSTINA   Shhhh! Get away from here!

MARTÍN   [*Going closer*]   I have a few knickknacks that will interest you noble ladies.   [*He sticks his hand into the pouch he's carrying under his cape.*]

ISABEL   It's that beggar again. Be off!

AGUSTINA   [*Reaching into her bodice*]   If we don't give him something, he won't leave. Do you have a coin?   [*Doña Isabel shakes her head as she searches. Both look back toward the window with alarm.*]

MARTÍN   Look what fine slippers I have. You won't see a prettier pair . . .

ISABEL   You have no business with us, you rascal.

[*Doña Marcela de Ulloa appears behind them on the balcony. She is a duenna, a widow to judge by the black nun-like headdress that frames her full, youthful face. She is still attractive at forty; she is the rigorously vigilant guardian of the two Infantas.*]

AGUSTINA   Doña Marcela!

DOÑA MARCELA   [*In a cold, precise voice*]   My lord Don Diego Ruiz de Azcona, kindly assist me with these ladies.   [*To Isabel and Agustina*]   Could we know who gave you permission to go out on the balcony?   [*Don Diego Ruiz de Azcona, official escort to the Infantas, appears behind her. He is wearing a white ruff and black doublet with long, loose sleeves. He is in his fifties, and his gaunt face always has a distant, bored expression.*]

AGUSTINA   We saw the man who sells laces and ribbons and . . .

DOÑA MARCELA   Once it was a stray dog; then a young man standing in the street. You, Doña Isabel, are the eldest, and you should set a better example . . .

RUIZ DE AZCONA   They'll behave better from now on, I'm sure . . . Please go back in, ladies. Life is far more pleasant inside. When you get to my age, you'll understand that.   [*He steps aside, and the two girls go inside.*]

MARTÍN   [*Holding up the slippers*]   Noble lady: take a look at these lovely slippers with their gold trim . . .

DOÑA MARCELA   [*Raising her voice*]   Are there no guards in the palace?

MARTÍN   But, lady . . .

DOÑA MARCELA   [*To Azcona*]   One can't take a step outside these days without running into a plague of beggars.   [*Azcona agrees with a tired gesture.*]

DOÑA MARCELA   Guard! Over here!   [*Martín steps back, alarmed. Pedro turns his head, expectant. A Burgundian guard is at left, carrying a pike.*]   Get those disreputable men away from here!

PEDRO   [*Raising his head proudly*]   What did she say?

MARTÍN   [*Stepping back and taking him by the arm*]   There's no need, lady. We're going now . . .   [*He goes a few steps right under the watch of the guard who stops and rests his pike.*]

PEDRO [*Resisting*]   Leave me at Don Diego's door!

MARTÍN Later, brother. This isn't the time.

[*He heads him offstage right. Meanwhile the center curtains part (or lights come up) to reveal a room in the house of Velázquez. Martín and Pedro enter again from right. In the central area, Doña Juana Pacheco leans against a chair and looks toward the open door at right. She listens expectantly. Her dress is modest, without farthingale or hoops; her hair is arranged simply and is still dark although she is well into her fifties. Her figure has grown heavier with age but her face retains the appeal of a woman who, without being beautiful, was captivating. At her side, her son-in-law, Juan Bautista del Mazo, looks at her in silence. He is a thin man of forty-four and dresses in black with a ruff. The Burgundian guard lifts his pike and continues his round until he exits at right.*]*

DOÑA MARCELA [*With a furtive glance toward the Treasury House*]   Please send Doña Isabel back to me.

RUIZ DE AZCONA Be gentle with her. They're still young.

DOÑA MARCELA [*With a smile*]   Trust me to do what is best.   [*Azcona goes inside. Doña Marcela looks toward Velázquez's house.*]

JUANA Did you hear? He's put away his brushes and palette.

MAZO Do you think he'll let me see it?

JUANA Why does that painting interest you so much?

MAZO Doesn't it interest you?

JUANA [*With an ambiguous expression*]   I've seen a lot of his paintings over the years.   [*She continues to listen. Doña Isabel appears on the balcony.*]

DOÑA MARCELA Come here, Isabel. It's not forbidden to come out. . .as long as you do so with a person who commands proper respect. Enjoy the air a while with me.

ISABEL Thank you, señora.

DOÑA MARCELA [*Looking left*]   Isn't that the Moorish slave of Don Diego Velázquez?

ISABEL It is, señora. But he isn't a slave anymore.

DOÑA MARCELA   To be sure. The King has given him his freedom.

JUANA   [*Suddenly starting to walk around*]   You seem to be fascinated by his paintings. I'm more concerned with my grandchildren.

MAZO   Is that a reproach, señora?

JUANA   You should be careful with the little one . . . He's getting too fat.

MAZO   You mustn't worry about the child. We'll see that he doesn't eat too much.

JUANA   Shhhh! He's going out on the balcony now.

[*She stops and listens. Diego Velázquez appears on the balcony at right and leans on the railing with a sigh of relief. He is wearing the black suit, with open satin sleeves and narrow ruff in which he portrayed himself in the famous painting. On his belt the black key of the Chamberlain of the Royal Household. He is fifty-seven and retains in his appearance the unique combination of arrogance and simplicity that he always displayed. His face is smooth; the mustache black. There are touches of gray in his great mane of hair. He is absorbed in thought.*]

DOÑA MARCELA   Look. Don Diego is coming out on the balcony.

[*Juan de Pareja enters left, crosses, and stops under the balcony of the Treasury House. Pareja is about forty-six. His features are African and his complexion deep olive; his hair, mustache, and beard very dark. He is wearing a dark suit with a wide linen "Walloon" collar. At first Velázquez does not notice him, for he has shaded his eyes with one hand and is looking right.*]

PAREJA   Master . . .

VELÁZQUEZ   [*With an ironic smile*]   Master? Are you forgetting that the King has freed you?   [*His diction is soft and warm.*]

PAREJA   Forgive me, sir. I must speak with you.

VELÁZQUEZ   In a moment.   [*He looks right again using his hand as a visor. Pareja is about to enter through the front door.*]   Wait . . . look over toward the Cañon del Peral. Don't you see something different?

PAREJA   I don't see anything.

DOÑA MARCELA   What can they be looking at?

ISABEL   They say that people have been seeing two armies in the skies of Madrid...that it's a sign of a victory over the French. Do you suppose he can see things like that?

VELÁZQUEZ   Don't you see a new shadow?

PAREJA   On the right side?

VELÁZQUEZ   Yes, what is it?

PAREJA   I've heard that they're excavating in the Caños for a new building.

JUANA   What can he be doing out there?

MAZO   I thought I heard his voice.

[*Juana sits down, impatient.*]

VELÁZQUEZ   It's curious how little the tints of things tell us about them. I begin to wonder if they're not telling us a deeper truth.

PAREJA   What, sir?

VELÁZQUEZ   [*Looking at him with a smile*]   That they're not things at all, even though they seem so to us.

PAREJA   I don't understand, sir.

VELÁZQUEZ   Would you like to see what I've just finished?

PAREJA   [*Excited*]   Would you let me?

VELÁZQUEZ   Yes, you and my son-in-law. Both of you can come up.   [*Pareja hurries through the front door. Velázquez is about to leave the balcony when, intrigued, he looks into the distance again.*]

DOÑA MARCELA   [*Who hasn't taken her eyes off Velázquez*]   He's pretending not to see us.

ISABEL   Do you think so?

DOÑA MARCELA   He's a proud man. Has he used you again as a model for the sketch of the painting he's planning?

ISABEL   No. And you, señora?

DOÑA MARCELA   No, but our lady the Infanta María Teresa is often in his studio.

ISABEL   Is he painting her in my place?

DOÑA MARCELA   That's the curious part...he's not painting her at all.

ISABEL   Then what do they do?

DOÑA MARCELA   They talk. You know that the Infanta delights in talking...and thinking...It seems impossible that she's only your age. His Majesty doesn't know whether to rejoice or mourn. But I'm not one to question. An infanta can do things that are forbidden to attendants...Don Diego hasn't moved.

ISABEL   No...I'll be so happy when he has finished his painting.

DOÑA MARCELA   Why?

ISABEL   Then they'll put the furniture back for us. We used to have such wonderful times in the studio.

JUANA   Did someone knock?

MAZO   Yes, señora.

[*Azcona reappears behind Doña Marcela.*]

AZCONA   The Infanta Doña María Teresa is on her way to see her august sister.

DOÑA MARCELA   Heaven help us! And here we are committing the ugliest sin of all.

ISABEL   What sin is that?

DOÑA MARCELA   Looking at a man too much. Now you see the dangers of balconies. Run fetch your vihuela, Doña Isabel. You know how much she likes to hear you play...

[*They exit from the balcony, followed by Azcona, as Pareja enters the central area and kisses Doña Juana's hand.*]

PAREJA   God keep my lady. My lord Don Diego is giving his permission to Don Juan Bautista and this humble servant to view his new canvas!

MAZO   Has he already finished it?

PAREJA   He told me so from the balcony.

[*Mazo goes quickly to the door at right.*]

MAZO   Maestro, can we come up?

[*Velázquez answers from the balcony door toward the interior.*]

VELÁZQUEZ Haven't you been paying us regular visits for a week now?

MAZO I was eager to see the painting.

VELÁZQUEZ Then come up. [*He exits from the balcony and Mazo exits right.*]

PAREJA With your leave, señora. [*He exits behind Mazo. Juana watches them coldly. Then she gets up and goes to the door to listen.*]

VELÁZQUEZ [*From offstage*] We have enough light now.

[*He crosses right behind the balcony window. Mazo and Pareja are glimpsed following him. Then they stop in amazement at what they see. From offstage left, Doña Isabel begins to play the "Second Pavan" of Milán on her vihuela. Pareja is about to step in front of Mazo to get a closer look at the painting but catches himself in time and steps back.*]

PAREJA Forgive me.

MAZO No, no...Do come closer. [*Mazo moves nearer the offstage painting, disappearing from view. Pareja takes a few steps and disappears in turn. A long pause. Mazo reappears and stands against the balcony door.*] It's incredible.

PAREJA'S VOICE Not even Titian could have painted anything like this.

VELÁZQUEZ'S VOICE Maybe the model's beauty has clouded your artistic judgment.

[*Doña Juana, with an expression of disapproval, exits center.*]

MAZO Titian's models were not so beautiful, Don Diego. [*He comes out on the balcony and leans against the railing in thought. Velázquez reappears, smiling.*] I'd like to copy it someday.

VELÁZQUEZ That could be dangerous for you...Juan, what are you doing in there gaping like an idiot? You'll have plenty of time to see it. Let's go down now. [*He disappears from view. Mazo enters and looks at the invisible painting again. Pareja reappears, stepping back from the canvas.*] Shall we go, my sons? [*After a final glance, both disappear from view. Their voices are heard from the stairs. The Burgundian guard enters again from right and crosses slowly, exiting left.*] What were you coming to tell me, Juan?

PAREJA'S VOICE   Forgive me, sir. Your painting made me forget. The head sweeper was looking for you because his helpers refuse to clean the North Gallery.

[*The music stops. Velázquez enters the central area through the door at right. Mazo follows, still absorbed in thought. Then Pareja enters and continues talking with Velázquez.*]

VELÁZQUEZ   And what about it?   [*Juana enters again upstage center.*]

PAREJA   They're asking for their back wages. They wanted to go directly to the Marqués. It would be better if you forestalled that.

VELÁZQUEZ   I wouldn't think of interfering. Let them protest to the Marqués. . .Sit down, Juana, we must talk.   [*He leads her to a chair and sits near her.*]   Bautista, my son, what are you thinking about so intently?

MAZO   [*With a faint smile, pointing toward the workroom*]   Do you realize that it is the first time a Spaniard has dared to do that?   [*Juana looks down.*]

VELÁZQUEZ   Let's hope it's not the last.

JUANA   God will it's the last!

VELÁZQUEZ   Juana, why do you say that?

JUANA   Forgive me.

VELÁZQUEZ   Take the key.   [*He hands it to her.*]   It won't be necessary for you to clean the workroom any longer. In a few days I'll put the painting away, and you can leave the room open again.   [*He stands.*]   I'm counting on your silence.

MAZO   Of course, Don Diego.

VELÁZQUEZ   [*To Mazo*]   Go on to the palace. And you, Juan, wait for me outside. We'll go together.

[*Pareja bows and exits.*]

MAZO   May God keep you.   [*He exits.*]

JUANA   Go with God, Bautista.

VELÁZQUEZ   Can I trust you? And them?

JUANA   How can you doubt it?

VELÁZQUEZ They are painters.

JUANA They are devoted to you.

VELÁZQUEZ It's sad not to know how to go on without showing what we paint. It's not vanity: it's just that we always paint for someone... whom we never find. [*He slowly takes his left hand in his right and presses down on it in a gesture that Juana does not fail to notice. Concerned, she gets up and goes to his side.*]

JUANA [*Taking his arm affectionately*] You're not alone, Diego.

VELÁZQUEZ I know that, Juana. [*He takes his arm away and goes to the armchair.*] I have you, I have our grandchildren, every day the house fills with pupils who respect me, and the King honors me with his friendship. [*He smiles.*] I'm the most accompanied man in the world! [*He sits.*]

JUANA Then why do you feel alone?

VELÁZQUEZ [*Laughing*] It's my painting that feels alone.

JUANA [*Shaking her head sadly*] I know that in your eyes I'm just a poor woman who doesn't understand a thing about painting. Or about you...since you are your painting. [*She stands behind the armchair and gently caresses his hair.*]

VELÁZQUEZ Where did you get such ideas?

JUANA Let me say what's on my mind! Behind you, so you won't see... how old I've become.

VELÁZQUEZ You and I are almost the same age.

JUANA That's why I'm older. Women still look at you at court; it's obvious enough to me. And I'm only a grandmother doting on her grandchildren.

VELÁZQUEZ Not for me, Juana. [*He presses his left hand with his right again.*]

JUANA Then why do you feel alone...with me? Why are you so silent?

VELÁZQUEZ I've always been sparing of words.

JUANA You used to confide in me. You told me what made you happy and what made you sad. Then...

VELÁZQUEZ Then what?

JUANA   You took your second trip to Italy.   [*She steps back, pained.*]
You were gone a long time. And you came back...very changed.

VELÁZQUEZ   [*After a moment*]   When you breathe the air and experience
the light of Italy, Juana, you understand that until then you were a
prisoner...The Italians have a reputation for being secretive but
they're not sad hypocrites like us. Returning to Spain becomes an
unbearable thought, and time slips by...On my second trip, I
couldn't deny it any longer: I considered staying.

JUANA   Do you see?

VELÁZQUEZ   And bringing you there later. But that would have presented
difficulties...One always returns to Spain, in spite of everything.
It's not so easy to free myself from this land.   [*He presses his hand
again.*]

JUANA   But before, Diego, I was your confidante. I would sit beside
you...   [*She sits.*]   as now, and your hand would seek mine...
Look at your hands now. Since you came back, they only seek each
other...

VELÁZQUEZ   [*Her observation startles him, and he unclasps his hands.*]
What are you saying?

JUANA   What is your hand searching for, Diego?   [*Her arm slips down
and takes his hand.*]   Another woman?

VELÁZQUEZ   [*After a moment*]   There was no other woman, Juana.   [*He
gets up abruptly and takes a few steps.*]

JUANA   [*With a sudden boldness*]   What has been going on up there in
your workroom?

VELÁZQUEZ   I've been painting.

[*She bursts into tears.*]

I've painted, Juana! Get those ghosts out of your head!

JUANA   Then you must have a woman in the palace!

VELÁZQUEZ   [*Pressing his hands together in exasperation*]   You're losing
your mind!

JUANA   [*Pointing to his hands*]   Your hands again!

VELÁZQUEZ   [*Separating them brusquely*]   Maybe they're reaching out for
someone without my knowing it. But not another woman, as you

think. Someone to help me bear the torment of seeing clearly in this land of blindmen and lunatics. You're right: I am alone. But years ago I met someone who could have been like a brother. [*With a bitter smile*] He knew what life was. That's why things went badly for him. He was a beggar.

JUANA   Who was?

VELÁZQUEZ   I don't even remember his name. He's probably dead now. Forgive me, Juana. I am alone but I do have you. [*He goes to her side and lifts her chin.*] I shouldn't have raised my voice. It's only that I'm uneasy about the painting I want so much to begin. The King must authorize it, and I don't know if he will.

JUANA   Will you swear by your faith that there's . . . no other woman?

VELÁZQUEZ   Why must you be so childish? [*He moves away from her.*]

JUANA   You haven't sworn!

VELÁZQUEZ   Shhhh! Didn't someone come in?

[*Juan de Pareja enters from upstage. He is bringing Velázquez's sword, cloak, and hat.*]

PAREJA   Your cousin Don José Nieto begs to be received by my lady. I brought your things in case you wanted to avoid him.

VELÁZQUEZ   [*Smiling*]   Clever of you. Wait for me at the door. I'll slip out by the hallway.

[*Pareja nods. Juana takes the things he has brought and puts them on a chair. Pareja exits upstage. Juana helps her husband buckle on the sword and put on his cloak in silence. At the same time, Doña Marcela comes out on the left balcony and surveys the street, looking furtively toward the Treasury House. Ruiz de Azcona looks out a moment later.*]

DOÑA MARCELA   It's a cool day. The Infanta can take her stroll.

RUIZ DE AZCONA   Shall we go then?

DOÑA MARCELA   Please start without me. I have an urgent message to deliver to the Treasury House . . .

RUIZ DE AZCONA   If you prefer, another duenna can accompany us . . .

DOÑA MARCELA   It will only take a moment. I'll be right along . . .

RUIZ DE AZCONA   We'll be in the Prioress Garden.

[*Both exit from the balcony.*]

JUANA   Why do you avoid your cousin?

VELÁZQUEZ   He always talks like a child.

JUANA   To you we're all children.

VELÁZQUEZ   Perhaps...

JUANA   He's the best friend you have in the palace, Diego.

VELÁZQUEZ   Then why did he solicit the post of Head Chamberlain to the King when I had requested it?

JUANA   He explained that to you: others were presenting themselves and it was better for him to get the appointment if they didn't give it to you. He cares for you very much, Diego.

VELÁZQUEZ   You more than me. I don't object, since you enjoy his idle talk. With your leave, I'll slip out.   [*He kisses her on the forehead.*]   Wish me luck, Juana. Maybe the King will make up his mind today.

JUANA   I'll say a prayer for you!   [*He presses her hands, takes his hat, and exits right. Juana watches him leave, sighs, and then exits upstage. Meanwhile, the Infanta María Teresa comes out on the left balcony and looks wistfully toward the Treasury House. She is only eighteen, but there is something in her features that makes her seem older. She has inherited her father's ash-blonde hair, the thick lower lip, and a slightly protruding chin; but her expression is gentle and penetrating, her movements quick. She is wearing a luxurious tight bodice with hoopskirt. The heavy court hairdo seems light and elegant on her graceful head. She is watching her little sister start her walk and waves to her affectionately. Then she steps back inside. Velázquez and Pareja come onstage through the main door of the Treasury House. Doña Marcela enters left and meets them as they cross. Reverences are exchanged.*]

VELÁZQUEZ   [*Taking off his hat*]   Señora...

DOÑA MARCELA   God keep you, Don Diego. I must give you a message.

VELÁZQUEZ   Here?

DOÑA MARCELA   It's a small matter.

VELÁZQUEZ You may go on, Juan.   [*Pareja bows and exits left. A short silence*]   Well?

DOÑA MARCELA [*Speaking with difficulty*]   Not this way, Don Diego. Don't make it more difficult for me.

VELÁZQUEZ I don't understand what you mean.

DOÑA MARCELA But you do understand. And even if you didn't, you shouldn't speak to me so formally . . . We've known each other since you were under the protection of the Count-Duke of Olivares and I served in his house. I was hardly more than a child then . . . a young girl courted by a great many handsome young men . . . while I only yearned for a true friendship.

VELÁZQUEZ Are you referring to the time when your husband was still living?

DOÑA MARCELA Don't speak his name! You know quite well that I was married against my will. It was a cross I had to bear.

[*The Infanta María Teresa reappears on the balcony and observes them cautiously from the doorway without going to the railing.*]

VELÁZQUEZ To be sure, I remember that you honored me with that confidence.

DOÑA MARCELA I came to believe that you had forgotten it. You seemed so busy loving your wife.

VELÁZQUEZ So I was.

DOÑA MARCELA [*With a tender look*]   But you do remember it.

VELÁZQUEZ Remembering the past is what old people do best, señora.

DOÑA MARCELA A man like you is never old, Don Diego.

VELÁZQUEZ Or young . . . Forgive me; I'm expected at the palace. Your servant, Doña Marcela.   [*He bows and starts left.*]

DOÑA MARCELA Don't go yet!

VELÁZQUEZ Señora . . .

DOÑA MARCELA Shhh!   [*The guard crosses from left to right. Doña Marcela steps closer to Velázquez.*]   Why do you refuse to understand? Doesn't a woman's suffering arouse a little pity in you? Are you made of ice?

VELÁZQUEZ   Señora, your moral rectitude is proverbial in the palace. How could one so impeccable abandon herself to the greatest of sins? I cannot believe it.

DOÑA MARCELA   [*Faintly*]   It's the most human of all.

VELÁZQUEZ   I speak, señora, of the sin of duplicity. No doubt you want to have your little joke at my expense.

DOÑA MARCELA   [*Eyes down*]   Don't make me ashamed of myself.

VELÁZQUEZ   I want to warn you that we're being watched.   [*Doña Marcela looks right.*]   It's not the guard, señora. It's the Infanta María Teresa.

DOÑA MARCELA   Ah. . .   [*She composes herself.*]   They say she frequents your studio. Are you painting her portrait?

VELÁZQUEZ   Not yet.   [*He bows.*]   Your servant, Doña Marcela.

DOÑA MARCELA   [*Smiling and returning the reverence*]   Beware of rejected women, Don Diego.

[*She exits right. Velázquez puts on his hat and exits left. Neither of them has looked toward the balcony where María Teresa now peers out to watch them separate. Then she disappears from view. Meanwhile, Juana reappears upstage, followed by José Nieto Velázquez, cousin of the painter. He is a short, curt man of forty-five, with a large nose and shifty eyes. He is prematurely balding, with a wisp remaining on top. He is dressed in black from head to foot, with a ruff and cape, just as we see him in the painting "Las Meninas."*]

JUANA   We can be more at ease here. . .

NIETO   I should be speaking with your husband; but you always listen to me with more courtesy than he. . .

JUANA   He always has his mind on his work. But he cares for you. . . Is it something serious?   [*She sits and points to the other chair. Nieto remains standing.*]

NIETO   I don't think so. . . though one should always be on guard. His Majesty's painters have been gossiping. It wouldn't surprise me if they tried to put Don Diego in disfavor with the King.

JUANA   I've always told my husband that you are our best friend.

NIETO   I try to be, most humbly.   [*He sits near her.*]

JUANA   [*With a sudden urgency in her voice*]   Do what you can for him, cousin! He needs your help.

NIETO   Do you say this for some special reason?

JUANA   No, no. . .

NIETO   From the tone of your voice, I thought. . .

[*Juana shakes her head and smiles sadly. She gets up, perturbed. Nieto is about to get up too.*]

JUANA   Don't get up. . .I'm all right. . .Tell me all the latest news. . . What do you know about the miraculous discovery at Balchín del Hoyo?

NIETO   Canon Barrionuevo was telling me yesterday after the novena that they've found a buried castle and reached a pair of iron doors that may guard the treasure.

JUANA   How do they know there's a treasure?

NIETO   A laborer dreamed about it every night for two weeks, and he showed them exactly where to dig. . .   [*Sadly*]   But we shouldn't be too quick to believe it. Satan knows that Spain is favored by the Blessed Virgin, and he plots against us always.

JUANA   May Our Lord keep us free from his power!   [*She crosses herself.*]

NIETO   It's certain that we need all his grace not to fall into the snares of the Enemy. . .   [*Juana sits down again.*]   He always knows a way to attack. A prideful thought, envy of another's possessions, an immodest woman. . .

JUANA   [*With a start*]   A woman?

NIETO   You know very well that's one of his oldest tricks. And more dreadful than you may think, for sometimes such a woman is but the devil himself who takes her form to bewitch the man and destroy his home.

JUANA   And. . .how does one know if it is the devil or simply a woman?

NIETO   There are procedures, exorcisms. . .They are used according to the circumstances.

JUANA Yes, of course. [*A pause. Suddenly she starts to cry.*]

NIETO Señora! [*Juana tries to dry her tears. Nieto stands.*]

JUANA Forgive me. I'm out of sorts today.

NIETO I don't doubt that something's troubling you . . . You know you can confide in me.

JUANA I know that, but . . .

NIETO What's to stop you? It's obvious that I feel only good will toward you.

JUANA [*Without looking at him*] Swear that you'll tell no one what I'm going to tell you in confidence.

NIETO Is it so important?

JUANA [*Nodding*] Swear to me.

NIETO In all that does not go against my conscience I swear to keep silent.

JUANA I don't know how to begin . . .

NIETO Is it something to do with your husband? [*Juana nods.*] And you? [*She nods again.*] Perhaps . . . a woman?

JUANA Do you know something? Is there some lady of the court?

NIETO I don't think so . . .

JUANA Then it's the one who comes here!

NIETO What do you mean?

JUANA He has promised me that she won't come back. But I know that I haven't mattered to him for years . . . They were always together upstairs, with the door closed. He said he was only painting . . .

NIETO A woman . . . from the street?

JUANA Yes.

[*Martín and Pedro enter right and sit downstage on the steps. Martín takes a crust of bread from his pouch, divides it, and gives a piece to Pedro. They eat.*]

NIETO And you fear . . . some diabolic influence?

JUANA I don't know what I fear.

NIETO Could I see that painting?

JUANA No! I can't show it to you! The room is locked.

NIETO Locked? Haven't you seen it?

JUANA I can't show it! He has forbidden me!

[*Nieto hesitates and then takes her hand.*]

NIETO I can't be of much help to you if I don't see the painting.

JUANA I don't want to disobey him. I mustn't betray him.

NIETO Describe it to me.

JUANA [*After a moment, with a display of great modesty and repugnance*] I don't dare. [*A silence. Nieto frowns, suspects the truth, and goes upstage.*]

NIETO I'll think about the matter, señora. With your leave, I'll go. God keep you. [*He starts to exit.*]

JUANA [*Frightened in the face of his sudden departure*] Don't go! [*Nieto pauses. In the midst of a great inner struggle, Juana gets up and goes right. She places her hand on the doorknob and speaks without looking directly at Nieto.*] Come up with me. [*She opens the door and exits, followed by Nieto.*]

MARTÍN Get away from here, dog! You're full of fleas.

PEDRO There's no dog around here.

MARTÍN You see, ladies and gentlemen? Crazy and blind as a bat. [*Pedro is about to get up. Martín stops him and speaks to him affectionately.*] Have you eaten your bread?

PEDRO No.

MARTÍN There's nothing left in the pouch. You can search it.

PEDRO No need for that.

MARTÍN Do you want me to wait for you?

PEDRO [*Getting up*] No. Just show me the way. [*Martín gets up too and leads him to the door of the Treasury House.*]

MARTÍN Think it over. There's still time.

PEDRO [*Embracing him*] Good luck, Martín.

MARTÍN   Good luck to you.   [*Pedro enters the main door of Velázquez's house. Martín watches and then, sighing, exits right. Juana comes into view in the window of the right balcony and steps aside to let Nieto pass. He stops for a moment to look at the invisible painting.*]

NIETO   Dear God!   [*He moves from view to go closer to the painting. Juana, greatly distressed, follows him and disappears from sight. At the same time, the light on the central area dims, the upstage curtains part, and the light comes up again to reveal Velázquez's studio in the palace. Upstage left, the door is open. Pareja opens the shutters of the further-most balcony window and then comes downstage to open those of the second one. The room fills with light. Meanwhile, Maestro Angelo Nardi enters through the half-open door at right and watches Pareja. He is an elderly man of seventy-two, bald, with a silvery goatee which creates a strange contrast with his youthful clothes of brilliant and unusual colors. Perhaps a trace of his native Florentine accent can be detected in his very careful speech.*]

NARDI   Am I disturbing you?

PAREJA   Not at all, Maestro Nardi.

NARDI   Since the room was open, I thought I'd stretch my legs a bit. It's very confining in there.

PAREJA   [*Going to the desk and starting to select brushes*]   I'm at your command, maestro.   [*Nardi goes to the easel. Pareja keeps his eye on him.*]

NARDI   Have you seen the Saint Jerome I'm painting for Alcalá?

PAREJA   I haven't had an opportunity yet.

NARDI   I value your opinion, because I'm getting old. I think one should learn from the younger painters.

PAREJA   I'm only an apprentice, maestro.

NARDI   What? I say that you paint very well, my boy. And I'm sure there are others who would say the same.   [*He looks at the outline on the canvas.*]

PAREJA   With your permission.   [*He puts a folding seat in front of the canvas. Nardi steps back quickly.*]

NARDI   Of course, my boy.   [*Pareja sets up another seat beside the folding chair where he places the palette, brushes, a painter's maulstick, and a cloth. Nardi points to the canvas.*]   A strange whim, don't you think?

PAREJA So it is, maestro.

NARDI No one else would think of transferring so trivial a subject to such an enormous size. [*He points to a very large frame that rests against the wall.*] But he. . .he has thought of it. We will just have to accept it. . .as some other things have been accepted. He is such a good man!

PAREJA He is the finest man in the world, maestro.

NARDI Indeed he is. Envious people say that his goodness is only pretense, but we know his great heart, and we let him have his way. He wants to be alone in this gallery? Well, we other painters are very happy to work in the adjoining room and give him that pleasure.

PAREJA That reminds me that I must close up the room now. Your Grace will surely forgive me. . .

[*Nardi decides not to hear and takes a few short steps to snoop in the paints on the desk.*]

NARDI Don Diego must have ways to make himself loved if you don't resent all the years you spent learning to paint secretly, so that he would not be angry at you. . .That is proof of his goodness. . .

PAREJA [*Impatient*] So it is, maestro. If you don't mind, I'll close the doors now. [*He goes to lock the door at upstage left.*]

NARDI Go right ahead, my boy. I'll be on my way.

[*When Pareja starts to close the other door, the Marqués appears in the doorway. He is well into his fifties, with short hair in the fashion of the previous reign and full mustaches. He wears at his waist the golden key of a gentleman and on his breast the insignia of the Order of Santiago. His manner is arrogant; his voice that of a man used to giving orders.*]

PAREJA [*Bowing*] I kiss Your Excellency's hands.

MARQUÉS You're going to lock this room again?

PAREJA If Your Excellency does not object. . .

MARQUÉS Do you intend to impede the passage of His Majesty's Chief Steward? Has your new freedom gone to your head?

PAREJA [*Stepping back*] I beg Your Excellency's pardon.

MARQUÉS You may leave. [*Pareja hesitates.*] Without locking the door! [*Pareja bows and exits. The Marqués steps forward.*] As arrogant as his master. God keep you, maestro. [*Nardi bows.*] Have they been evading my orders?

NARDI [*Prudently closing the door at right*] They close off the room only on occasion, Your Excellency.

MARQUÉS But they do close it. Obviously no one except the Lord Chamberlain Velázquez gives orders in the King's quarters. They still don't know who I am, and by God they're going to learn.

NARDI [*Cautiously*] Before or after he does the painting?

MARQUÉS I don't know yet, maestro. I have to wait for the right moment to speak to the King.

NARDI I was asking because, with all respect, I don't know if Your Excellency has noticed what Don Diego wants to paint.

MARQUÉS [*Standing before the easel*] This?

NARDI That is a sketch of it. My own modest judgment leads me to believe that it's going to be frightfully scandalous. And for Velázquez's own sake . . . it would be better, perhaps, that he not continue with the painting.

MARQUÉS Explain what you mean.

NARDI Now now, Excellency . . . It's something to speak of at a more propitious time . . . [*He indicates to the Marqués with a gesture that they are being observed. Velázquez has appeared in the upstage door and stands there a moment. Then he leaves his hat, cloak, and sword on the desk and joins them. Pareja appears in turn upstage and slips into the room.*]

VELÁZQUEZ [*With a bow*] God keep Your Graces.

[*Two short bows greet him.*]

NARDI God keep you, Lord Chamberlain.

VELÁZQUEZ Could Your Excellency grant me a moment of his attention?

MARQUÉS I have urgent matters to attend to.

VELÁZQUEZ This matter is urgent too. The palace sweepers are dissatisfied. I've tried to convince them but it's no use.

MARQUÉS Convince them of what?

VELÁZQUEZ To go back to work.

MARQUÉS What?

VELÁZQUEZ The North Gallery hasn't been cleaned even at this hour.

MARQUÉS They are nothing but urchins from the street . . . are they or are they not paid to sweep?

VELÁZQUEZ They are, Excellency.

MARQUÉS Then let them sweep!

VELÁZQUEZ They haven't received their wages for three months. And for five days now they've not gotten their food ration either.

[*The Dominican Friar appears in the upstage door, stops, and watches them.*]

MARQUÉS And what of that?

VELÁZQUEZ It is natural that Your Excellency not understand their extreme need, given Your Excellency's growing wealth.

MARQUÉS [*He steps forward, flushed.*] What are you referring to?

VELÁZQUEZ [*Calmly*] To Your Excellency's growing wealth.

NARDI [*Noticing the Dominican*] Excuse me, Your Graces . . .

[*He crosses rapidly between them to meet the Dominican.*]

Your Reverence can come this way; the door is open.

[*The Dominican enters smiling.*]

I hope my Saint Jerome is to your liking.

[*They come downstage. The others have bowed and the Dominican dispenses quick blessings without stopping.*]

This way, father, this way.

[*He holds open the door at right and the Dominican exits.*]

I kiss your hands, gentlemen.

[*The Marqués bows. Nardi exits, closing the door behind him.*]

VELÁZQUEZ What is Your Excellency's decision?

MARQUÉS   Understand one thing, Don Diego. Such discontent cannot exist in the palace; therefore, it doesn't exist.

VELÁZQUEZ   But it does.

MARQUÉS   Those rabble will do their work as soon as you exercise the authority you seem to lack. You resolve the problem!   [*He starts to exit.*]

VELÁZQUEZ   It's already resolved.

MARQUÉS   Are you trying to joke with me?

VELÁZQUEZ   No! But there's no need for you to worry. Those lads are on the palace ledgers as sweepers; therefore they sweep.

MARQUÉS   I swear to God, Chamberlain, that I'll teach you to speak properly to a noble who wears the Cross of Santiago!

VELÁZQUEZ   [*Wounded, he looks down at his own doublet where there is no cross.*]   I can only say one thing: there are those who are honored by wearing the cross and others who honor it by wearing it.

[*The Marqués takes a step toward him, but Velázquez stands his ground. The Marqués abruptly turns his back on him and starts upstage. He stops and turns around.*]

MARQUÉS   His Majesty orders you to wait here during the afternoon. He will come to see the sketch for your painting.

[*He exits upstage without deigning to respond to Pareja's reverence. Velázquez sighs and, facing the proscenium, presses one of his hands against the other. Pareja goes to his side.*]

PAREJA   The palette is ready, maestro.

VELÁZQUEZ   There are days when I marvel at my own stupidity.   [*He relaxes and goes to the easel.*]

PAREJA   Shall I close the door?

VELÁZQUEZ   Yes. But don't lock it.

[*Pareja goes upstage and closes the door.*]

The large painting can't be as severe as this. This rough outline may not please the King. It's disturbing to look at.

[*With a sigh of vexation, he sits down, takes up the palette, and attacks the canvas with determination. Pareja begins to open the shutters.*]

Have you been to the places where the other painters gather to talk? What are they saying?

[*Pareja turns around in surprise.*]

Tell me.

PAREJA Maestro...why, you never wanted me to tell you before.

VELÁZQUEZ Because we were always in danger, and it's better not to know...Except at certain times. This painting is in danger now, and that does matter to me. Tell me and don't leave out the worst part.

PAREJA [*Clearing his throat*] Young Herrera bet the other painters ten ducats that the King would forbid you to paint it. He described it quite well for someone who hasn't seen it. He said it was a piece of nonsense...

VELÁZQUEZ It all comes from old Nardi and that wasps' nest in there. [*He points to the door at right.*] Continue. [*He paints.*]

PAREJA They saw me, and Herrera said that you were too proud of your-self for someone who painted so badly...and that it would be doing a favor to your immortal soul if someone told you so.

VELÁZQUEZ What a tiresome boy! He acts as if he were ninety years old: he talks exactly like the old painters.

PAREJA Someone chimed in to wager I wouldn't repeat any of this to you, considering how badly you treated me before the King freed me. They all said I'd done the right thing staying on with you. That way I was certain to get ahead.

VELÁZQUEZ Well, they offended you with the greatest piety. How did they tell your story?

PAREJA Like everyone else. That I learned secretly during all those years, because you would never permit a slave to paint. That I left a canvas of mine where the King would discover it, and that His Maj-esty forced you to free me after he saw it.

[*Both laugh.*]

VELÁZQUEZ I think that people will go on repeating that nonsense for a few centuries. It must be obvious that you could never have learned so much, living your whole life in my house, without my knowing it. But men will willingly believe the greatest stupidity provided they can belittle you with it.

PAREJA [*Lowering his voice*]   Even His Majesty believed it, sir.

VELÁZQUEZ [*Lowering his too*]   It was good that he did. Juan, my son: no man should be the slave of another.

PAREJA You never treated me as a slave, sir.

VELÁZQUEZ Because that was what I believed when I received you from my father-in-law. But if I had set you free, the Marqués, and all those who think as he does, would never have forgiven me. Did they say anything else?

PAREJA I really couldn't defend you . . . They were all of noble blood and old Christians, and I'm neither. So I decided to walk away . . .

[*Velázquez gets up to test something from downstage, with his back to the audience.*]

VELÁZQUEZ Juan, I think I'm going to be able to do the painting.

PAREJA You should have no doubts, sir.

VELÁZQUEZ If the King gives his consent, of course. Take the palette.

[*Pareja takes it, along with the brushes, and puts them on the chair.*]

PAREJA I don't know if I should tell you this, sir . . .

VELÁZQUEZ There's more?

PAREJA Not from the painters . . . but from your house.

VELÁZQUEZ Tell me.

PAREJA [*Not looking at him directly*]   Yesterday Doña Juana asked me if there was some woman . . . that you like. And if there had been another woman . . . in Italy. I said no.

[*A silence*]

VELÁZQUEZ That's good, Juan. Put everything away.

[*Pareja complies. The door upstage left opens and the Infanta*]

*María Teresa enters. She immediately closes the door behind her.
Velázquez and Pareja bow deeply.*]

Your Highness...

MARÍA TERESA [*She smiles, with a finger on her lips.*] Shhhh! I have
escaped from ceremony again.

VELÁZQUEZ Your Highness is very kind to prefer the conversation of a
poor painter.

[*He looks at Pareja who bows silently and starts to exit upstage.
The Infanta, in front of the easel, gives Velázquez a sly look.*]

MARÍA TERESA You're very modest. Don't leave, Pareja. When are you
beginning the large painting, Don Diego?

VELÁZQUEZ When His Majesty gives his consent.

MARÍA TERESA Did you say that I would be here?

VELÁZQUEZ His Majesty indicated that Your Highness would appear in
place of Doña Isabel de Velasco, if the painting is to be.

MARÍA TERESA And will you do that?

VELÁZQUEZ If it pleases Your Highness...

MARÍA TERESA [*She goes to the window of the first balcony. A moment of
silence.*] It pleases me. Tell me, Pareja: how did you manage to
paint all those years without Don Diego finding out?

[*The two men exchange concerned looks. She turns around.*]

I judge it impossible.

PAREJA I...stole hours from my sleep, Highness.

MARÍA TERESA [*Looking at them*] I see.

[*She goes to the easel and picks up the palette and brushes. With a
laugh.*]

May I?

VELÁZQUEZ Of course, Highness.

MARÍA TERESA [*She touches the brush to the canvas.*] Is this the way?

VELÁZQUEZ It is one way.

MARÍA TERESA Pareja, you can do me the kindness to leave us now.

[*Pareja bows and exits upstage, closing the door behind him. María Teresa puts down the palette.*]

Are you my friend, Don Diego?

VELÁZQUEZ   I am your most loyal servant.

MARÍA TERESA   [*Curtly*]   Leave off the formalities. We're alone.

VELÁZQUEZ   Even so, I cannot...

MARÍA TERESA   Of course you can. Or don't you remember?

VELÁZQUEZ   Remember?

MARÍA TERESA   I do. I think I was probably six. Does it come back to you now?

VELÁZQUEZ   [*Amazed*]   Highness...

MARÍA TERESA   They left me alone with you for a moment, and you picked me up in your arms.

VELÁZQUEZ   [*Embarrassed*]   I never thought you could remember it.

MARÍA TERESA   You committed with a royal person the most serious error. You know that no one can ever touch us. Sometimes I've wondered if you did it as the protest of a man who doesn't consider himself inferior to anyone.

VELÁZQUEZ   I did it because I love children.

MARÍA TERESA   [*Gently*]   Forget who I am again: I'm still a child who doesn't know about anything. Children are always lied to at court. But I want to know. I want to know! And I turn to you.

VELÁZQUEZ   Your Highness has often honored me with her questions...

MARÍA TERESA   Today I shall ask another of my childhood friend. Because I know that he is the most discreet man in the palace. I'm also inclined to say the finest. Pareja could swear to that, I think.

VELÁZQUEZ   Your insight, Highness, is surprising for one of your age.

MARÍA TERESA   [*Sighing*]   My insight hasn't made me very happy, believe me. Would you answer what I ask without lying?

VELÁZQUEZ   [*Hesitating*]   I don't know if I'll be able to...

MARÍA TERESA   Without lying, Don Diego! There are already enough lies in this place!... Try to understand me.

VELÁZQUEZ   I think I do. . . I'll answer without lying.

MARÍA TERESA   You know that I often walk through the palace alone. My father scolds me, but something tells me that I must do it. Sometimes I catch a glimpse of a world that is not mine. . . the simple tenderness in the eyes of a washwoman, the tired look of a guard. I overhear people talking about a child with a fever, or a harvest that will be good this year. But they see me and become silent. Yesterday I listened to two veterans of the guard talking, but I don't know if what they said was anything more than the rumors that go around. . . You won't deceive me.

VELÁZQUEZ   Tell me.

MARÍA TERESA   Is it true that my father has had more than thirty natural children?

VELÁZQUEZ   All this can be very dangerous. . . for both of us.

MARÍA TERESA   I'm brave. And you?

VELÁZQUEZ   Not always.

MARÍA TERESA   Are you refusing to answer?

VELÁZQUEZ   How can I talk of these things to a young girl?

MARÍA TERESA   I'm going to be queen of France.

VELÁZQUEZ   You're eighteen years old. I'm fifty-seven. If they found out I was telling you the truth, no one would understand. Truth is a terrible burden. . . You may despise me for it one day.

MARÍA TERESA   I want the truth. Help me, Don Diego! I'm stifling in the court and I can only confide in you. My father always says: go talk with your attendants, go to the Queen. . . Sometimes I wonder if I'm sick. . . I'm as young or younger than they are and they seem like children to me. . . And my father. . . a child too. Only you seem like. . . a man. Won't you talk to me truthfully?

VELÁZQUEZ   [*After a moment*]   What you asked me is true.

[*The Infanta takes a deep breath. Then she sits in the armchair. Silence.*]

MARÍA TERESA   Isn't fidelity possible?

VELÁZQUEZ   Rarely.

MARÍA TERESA   Are men so despicable?

VELÁZQUEZ   They're...imperfect.

MARÍA TERESA   You're faithful.

VELÁZQUEZ   Do you believe that?

MARÍA TERESA   One knows. I'm certain.

VELÁZQUEZ   [*Going closer to her*]   We have to learn to forgive weaknesses...we all have them.

MARÍA TERESA   I know that I live in a world of sinners. But it's the lying that's so hard for me to forgive! When I pass in front of the portrait of King Louis, I have a habit of making a little joke of it. "I salute my future husband," I say, and my ladies laugh...But I'm thinking: What's in store for me? Maybe another bag of deceits and infidelity. Come closer. I want to dispense with etiquette now that we're alone.

[*She takes his hand. Velázquez trembles.*]

I give you my gratitude.

[*She withdraws her hand and speaks very softly.*]

If only King Louis...has some resemblance to you.

[*A series of loud knocks on the upstage door and then repeated.*]

VOICE OF NICOLASILLO   Don Diego, are you in there?

VOICE OF MARI BÁRBOLA   May we come in, Don Diego?

VELÁZQUEZ   It's the dwarfs.

MARÍA TERESA   Open the door. Open it.

[*Velázquez goes upstage and opens the door.*]

VOICE OF NICOLASILLO   Quiet, Lion! Don Diego, look how he obeys me! Lie down, Lion! That's an order.

[*Mari Bárbola makes a reverence and enters, waddling on her deformed legs. As she reaches the middle of the room, she bows before the Infanta. Nicolasillo, in the doorway, continues involved with the invisible dog.*]

VELÁZQUEZ   Aren't you going to greet Her Highness, Nicolasillo?

NICOLASILLO   Huh?

[*He sees the Infanta and enters, making a great reverence. Then he runs back to the door.*]

Lion, go away!

[*A frightening bark answers him. Scared, he runs to take refuge between Velázquez's legs.*]

Get away!. . . You see? He obeys me.

[*Pleased with himself, he steps forward. Mari Bárbola is a dwarf of indefinite age, blond, with a huge head. Perhaps she has a trace of a German accent in her nasal voice. Nicolasillo Pertusato, born in Italy, is a dwarf but he is also a child. He is no more than fourteen and appears a few years younger. The two are very different. She suffers from what is known today as achondroplasia, which is revealed in the large bones of her face, her stubby fingers, and limp. Nicolasillo is myxedemic and, because of his age, could be mistaken at times for a child. His limbs are fine and well proportioned; his head graceful and shapely, although its excessive size and a certain indefinable disharmony of features can be noticed. They are attractively dressed, just as we see them in the famous painting. Nicolasillo goes on with his conceited talk while Velázquez takes him by the shoulders and steers him toward the Infanta.*]

NICOLASILLO   He understands that I'm going to be a gentleman. Doesn't he, Infanta?

[*María Teresa gives him a distracted smile. Her thoughts are elsewhere.*]

MARI BÁRBOLA   You shouldn't ask so many questions. It's not becoming in servants.

NICOLASILLO   We are more than servants! Don Diego is going to paint us beside the Infanta Margarita because we are very important in this palace. Look, Mari Bárbola: look how ugly he's painting you! Just the way you are.

VELÁZQUEZ   Nicolas!

[*The Infanta reacts.*]

MARI BÁRBOLA   It doesn't matter. I'm used to it.   [*But she bites her lip and withdraws toward the balcony.*]

VELÁZQUEZ   Ask Mari Bárbola to forgive you.

NICOLASILLO   I will not.

VELÁZQUEZ   Then I will tell you something: I'm also going to put the dog in the painting, and he is less than a servant.

NICOLASILLO   [*After thinking about it*]   You're bad! Both of you!   [*He runs upstage.*]

VELÁZQUEZ   Come here.

NICOLASILLO   I won't. And when I grow up, the King will make you paint me as a gentleman, with big mustaches. And besides that, the dog's name is Lion. They'll call me Samson because he obeys me!

VELÁZQUEZ   Indeed! Don't they already call you "Lynx Eyes"?

NICOLASILLO   Because my eyes are sharp! Better than yours, lord painter. What do you see on that doorpost?

VELÁZQUEZ   Colors.

NICOLASILLO   Hah! Colors. There's a fly by the door.

VELÁZQUEZ   [*Smiling*]   Then maybe we should call you "Fly-Painter."

[*Mari Bárbola laughs. Nicolasillo gives her an angry look and turns to Velázquez.*]

NICOLASILLO   You don't want to admit that your eyes are weak. That's why you paint everything so fuzzy . . .

VELÁZQUEZ   Who says that?

NICOLASILLO   I don't know. I've heard it.

[*He inadvertently looks toward the door at right, and Velázquez notices. The Infanta stands; Nicolasillo runs to snoop in the paints; and Mari Bárbola joins him to scold him gently.*]

MARÍA TERESA   And what of these, Don Diego? There are more than fifty like them in the palace.

VELÁZQUEZ   [*Softly*]   They let them earn their living.

MARÍA TERESA   But not out of charity. Isn't that true?   [*A silence*]   Isn't it?

VELÁZQUEZ   The truth again.

MARÍA TERESA   Always.

VELÁZQUEZ   I don't believe it could be called charity.

[*Mari Bárbola has heard and is upset.*]

MARÍA TERESA   Thank you, Don Diego. Forgive my whims.

VELÁZQUEZ   Forgive *me* my sadness.

[*The Infanta starts upstage. Velázquez and the dwarfs make a reverence. She exits.*]

NICOLASILLO   What were you talking about?

MARI BÁRBOLA   Nicolasillo!

VELÁZQUEZ   [*He puts his hand on Nicolasillo's head affectionately.*]   About you. That you're a child and that I'll paint you as a child.

NICOLASILLO   Truly?

VELÁZQUEZ   Truly. So that when you're grown up, and I'm already dead, you'll say: I was a very beautiful child then.

[*Mari Bárbola is deeply affected and moves toward the balcony windows.*]

NICOLASILLO   You can also paint me listening. I know how to listen from a distance. Right now someone is going to come through that door.   [*He points upstage left. Pareja enters.*]   You see?   [*He jumps up and down with delight.*]

PAREJA   Forgive me, sir. Doña Juana is insisting that you come.

VELÁZQUEZ   What's wrong?

PAREJA   She is very frightened about a beggar who is looking for you and won't go away. I told her that you were waiting for His Majesty and that you would be late.

VELÁZQUEZ   Has no one helped the beggar?

PAREJA   Yes, but he fainted and seemed too weak to move on.   [*He smiles.*]   I'd say that he is an old acquaintance of yours, sir.

VELÁZQUEZ   Who?

PAREJA   That old rogue who was your model for "Aesop."

VELÁZQUEZ   What?

PAREJA   I'd swear that's who he is.

VELÁZQUEZ   [*To himself*]   Blessed God!   [*He goes hurriedly toward the door, picking up his hat, cloak, and sword on the way.*]

PAREJA   His Majesty is coming, sir!   [*But Velázquez looks at him without stopping and exits, followed by Pareja.*]

NICOLASILLO   No one's important enough for him to wait!

MARI BÁRBOLA   You were very rude to Don Diego.

NICOLASILLO   He called me a dog.

MARI BÁRBOLA   No he didn't. He's the only one who doesn't treat us like dogs.

NICOLASILLO   You can't complain. If you weren't here, you'd be in a carnival somewhere.

MARI BÁRBOLA   We're in a carnival here too.

NICOLASILLO   I'm not like you. I'm almost a man.   [*He strikes his breast.*]   Can't you see? When I'm tall as Don Diego and I marry the prettiest lady at court, you'll see who I am.

MARI BÁRBOLA   [*With tenderness*]   You'll never be as tall as Don Diego, Nicolasillo.

NICOLASILLO   You're a liar!

MARI BÁRBOLA   You'll never get married.

NICOLASILLO   Speak for yourself . . . with that face . . .

MARI BÁRBOLA   You're right. I'll never have a son to kiss either. You're still young . . . you don't understand yet . . . that we can only kiss the King's dogs.

NICOLASILLO   [*Almost shouting*]   I'll kiss whom I please!

MARI BÁRBOLA   Only the King's dogs . . .

NICOLASILLO   No! . . .   [*He breaks into sobs.*]

MARI BÁRBOLA   Nicolasillo, my son, forgive me. You are a beautiful child who will grow into a handsome man.

NICOLASILLO   I hate you!

MARI BÁRBOLA   No, you don't . . . And I care for you very much. I'll watch over you and protect you. Go on being an innocent child all your life . . . even after you're grown.

[*She puts her arms around him tenderly from behind.*]

You can be my son, if you wish . . . as long as I live.

[*She starts to kiss him on the cheek. Nicolasillo pulls away and turns on her.*]

NICOLASILLO   Go kiss the King's dogs!

[*Mari Bárbola slumps in a silent sob. A pause.*]

And don't cry.

[*Mari Bárbola controls herself.*]

Don't cry.

[*The lights dim slowly, and when they come up again, the area has become Velázquez's house. The painter enters from the rear and Juana almost simultaneously from right.*]

JUANA   Have you seen the King yet?

VELÁZQUEZ   Leave that for now. Where is the man?

JUANA   In the kitchen.

VELÁZQUEZ   Can he walk?

JUANA   He's able to stand up now. Who is he, Diego?

VELÁZQUEZ   Bring him here.

JUANA   [*She goes to the door and turns around.*]   He smells bad, he's dirty. He seems crazy . . . Get rid of him quickly, Diego! For the children's sake . . .

VELÁZQUEZ   Bring him.

[*Juana exits. He presses his hands together in tense expectation. Juana returns with Pedro and steps back. Pedro peers at the man in front of him. Velázquez looks at him fixedly.*]

God keep you, my friend.

PEDRO   Is it you, Don Diego? I don't see very well.

VELÁZQUEZ   It is.

PEDRO   Do you remember me?

VELÁZQUEZ   Of course. Don't you remember him, Juana? He was my model for "Aesop."

JUANA   That's . . . who he is?

PEDRO   It must have been fifteen years ago.

VELÁZQUEZ   How old are you now?

PEDRO   I don't remember anymore.

VELÁZQUEZ   Sit down.   [*He assists him.*]

JUANA   [*Shaking her head*]   Diego . . .

VELÁZQUEZ   Let us be alone, Juana.

PEDRO   Thank you, Don Diego.

> [*Juana starts to say something, but Velázquez gives her a look. She exits right with obvious annoyance.*]

VELÁZQUEZ   [*Closing the door*]   Now I remember your name: it's Pedro.

PEDRO   [*After a moment*]   Your memory is failing you . . . My name is Pablo.

VELÁZQUEZ   Pablo?

PEDRO   Yes. Pablo.

VELÁZQUEZ   [*Suspecting that Pedro has lied, he has a moment of doubt.*] Maybe I remember you as poorly as your name. Tell me what you want.

PEDRO   I don't even know . . . During all those years I thought of you often. Maybe I shouldn't have come.

VELÁZQUEZ   How has your life been?

PEDRO   A wanderer's life. And you?

VELÁZQUEZ   They promoted me to King's chamberlain. And I've painted.

PEDRO   [*He sighs.*]   You've painted . . .   [*A short silence*]   I should be going now.   [*He gets up. Both try to hide their embarrassment.*]

VELÁZQUEZ   Will you accept some help from me?

PEDRO   Your wife has already given me food. Thank you.

[*A pause. Velázquez presses his hands together.*]

Only one thing I'm curious about before I go. . . Then I'll leave you in peace.

VELÁZQUEZ   What is it?

PEDRO   Do you recall that you used to talk to me about your painting?

VELÁZQUEZ   [*Surprised*]   Yes.

PEDRO   One day you said: things change. . . Perhaps their truth is in their appearance, which also changes.

VELÁZQUEZ   Do you remember that?

PEDRO   I think you said: if we managed to look at them in a different way from the ancients, we could even paint a void. . . You also said that colors harmonize according to laws that you still didn't understand very well. Now do you know something of those laws?

VELÁZQUEZ   I think I do, more. . . Your memory amazes me! How can painting be so important to you if you don't paint?

[*A silence*]

PEDRO   [*With a sad smile*]   The fact is, Don Diego. . . I wanted to paint once.

VELÁZQUEZ   What?

PEDRO   I never told you then because I wanted to forget about painting. I haven't been able to forget. Now, as you see, I'm coming back to it. . . when I know I'll never paint.

VELÁZQUEZ   How little I know about you! Why haven't you painted?

PEDRO   I'll tell you about that in good time.

VELÁZQUEZ   Sit down.   [*He pushes him gently and sits beside him.*]   You should know that I'm getting ready to paint a canvas that will sum up all that I know. It won't resemble anything I've done. I now know that colors carry on a dialogue among themselves; that is the beginning of the secret.

PEDRO   A dialogue?

VELÁZQUEZ   I've done a sketch for the painting in the palace. Would you like to see it?

PEDRO   My sight is almost gone, Don Diego.

VELÁZQUEZ   Forgive me.

PEDRO   But I would like to see it, if you'll let me, before I leave you.

VELÁZQUEZ   [*Touching his arm*]   Pedro . . .

PEDRO   What?

VELÁZQUEZ   You kept many things hidden from me then; but you didn't lie to me. Your name is Pedro.

PEDRO   I see that you haven't changed. Forgive me. Life obliges us to do many strange things. I'll explain. I'm old, Don Diego. I don't have much time left, and I wonder what certainty the world has given me about anything . . . I just know that I'm sick of body, full of fear, and waiting for death. A tired man in search of a little sanity that will bring him a moment of peace from the insanity of other men before he dies.

VELÁZQUEZ   You will live here.

PEDRO   [*After a moment*]   Don't decide that yet.

VELÁZQUEZ   It's already decided! I'll leave you now and we can talk later. The King is coming to view my sketch. Maybe I've made him wait, and that would be very serious . . . It's up to him whether I paint the picture or not. But what you say about it matters to me more. Will you see it today? If you're not too exhausted . . .

PEDRO   I can walk.

VELÁZQUEZ   Then my servant Pareja will escort you in a half hour.

PEDRO   That slave of yours?

VELÁZQUEZ   The King has given him his freedom because he also paints. But I don't want to lie to you: Pareja and I achieved it through a trick.

PEDRO   And why was that?

VELÁZQUEZ   Have you forgotten your own words? No man should be a slave of another.

PEDRO   You make me feel young again, Don Diego.

VELÁZQUEZ   You didn't forget my painting either... Pedro. I know now that I am not painting only for myself.

PEDRO   Listen, keep on calling me Pablo in front of the others.

VELÁZQUEZ   As you wish...   [*He goes right and opens the door.*] Juana!... Juana!...

[*Juana enters. Pedro starts to get up with great effort.*]

Don't get up. You're sick.

[*Juana frowns at this unexpected deference.*]

I'm returning to the palace. This man will stay here for now. Tell Pareja to bring him to my studio in half an hour.

JUANA   Do I give him anything when he leaves?

VELÁZQUEZ   That won't be necessary, Juana. I'll be waiting for you in the palace... Pablo.

[*He exits upstage. Juana goes closer to Pedro and stares at him in silence. He returns her look with his tired eyes, hesitates, and finally gets up with effort. He remains standing before her with bowed head. The light fades on the two motionless figures, and the downstage curtain closes over the area. Then a high, cold light illuminates the downstage center area. Maestro Angelo Nardi enters right and waits. The Marqués appears from center and stations himself on the steps.*]

MARQUÉS   The council meeting is over. His Majesty approaches.

NARDI   Wouldn't it be best for you to speak to him alone?

MARQUÉS   Maestro Nardi, you understand painting better than I. Shhhh!

[*He points upstage center. Invisible hands separate the curtain to permit the entrance of Philip IV. At age fifty-one, the King looks tired and debilitated in spite of efforts to convey a more robust appearance. His pompadour is carefully arranged; the long ends of his mustache are waxed. Perhaps he dyes his hair, which is still ash blond. There is something repellent in his soft features and blank expression. Soberly dressed in black silk, he wears a ruff and the chain and insignia of the Order of the Golden Fleece on his breast.*]

He is wearing a short cloak, sword, and hat. When he appears, the
Marqués and Nardi kneel.]

KING   Rise.

MARQUÉS   Usher! Prepare a seat for His Majesty!

[*An usher enters carrying an armchair which he places downstage*
left. He bows and exits with a series of reverences.]

KING   [*With surprise*]   Weren't we going to the studio?

MARQUÉS   I dared to think that Your Majesty would wish to rest a
moment first.

KING   [*He comes down the steps and sits.*]   It's true, I am tired.

MARQUÉS   Your Majesty's great and serene spirit ought not suffer because
of the bad tidings from the council. Things have been worse before,
and God did not fail to help us.

KING   In Him I trust. But you know that seldom have we been in such
need of money. . . I waited a long time for that shipment of silver to
arrive: those six galleons loaded with wealth have been our life's
blood for years. . . Six galleons, Marqués! And the English have
sunk them! Meanwhile our troops go without food.   [*He removes*
his hat.]

MARQUÉS   They'll be able to live off the land.

KING   Perhaps. But there's a lack of military discipline. We've lost Portu-
gal and we're close to losing Catalonia. Peace would be better.

MARQUÉS   There'll be more silver coming from the Indies, sir.

KING   Yes. But how can we deal with our expenses until then. Merchants
are such common, vile persons. My word is not enough for them
anymore. . .

MARQUÉS   Raise taxes.

KING   Still more?

MARQUÉS   As much as necessary, sir! What greater obligation is there for
the people than to help their King continue to be the greatest monarch on earth? I must also give you some news that I didn't want to
bring out at the council, since it's not confirmed yet. But Your Majesty will no doubt be pleased.

KING   Yes?

MARQUÉS   In the town of Balchín del Hoyo they've discovered two bolted and padlocked doors in an old fortress. They have yet to be opened, but there must be a treasure behind them. Your Majesty will see how Providence comes to our aid.

KING   Let's hope it's God's will. In the meantime, if we raise taxes again, we might provoke more disturbances...

MARQUÉS   There can be no justification for riots against a king. Such discontent is a pernicious humor, a poisonous weed that must be uprooted without mercy. Fortunately Your Majesty has vassals capable of getting a whiff of the pestilent wind of rebellion...even when it blows in the palace.

KING   What do you mean by that?

MARQUÉS   It's not the first time that my loyalty forces me to stress this point in Your Majesty's presence. Rebellion is never more dangerous than when it wears the mask of humility.

KING   [Standing up]   Are you speaking of Velázquez?

MARQUÉS   That is correct, sir.   [The King paces. A pause.]

KING   Velázquez is no rebel.

MARQUÉS   In your presence, sir, no. He's not such a fool. But with me, from whom he receives just orders, he shows only disdain and disobedience.

KING   He is an excellent painter.

MARQUÉS   If Your Majesty will permit Maestro Nardi, also an excellent painter, to speak in my place, he will be able to point out some strange aspects of the painting that Velázquez intends to undertake.

KING   [After a moment]   Step forward, Maestro Nardi.

NARDI   [Coming forward and bowing.]   Sir...

KING   On another occasion, Carducho and you spoke to me unjustly of Velázquez. What do you have to tell me now? Measure your words carefully. Is it not a painting of the Infantas?

NARDI   But...not at all respectful of them...The lack of solemnity in their postures and attitudes makes them seem simply ladies of the court. The servants, the dwarfs, and even the dog seem no less important than the Infantas...   [*The King sits again. Nardi hesitates but goes on talking.*]   Neither is there a suitable background for the magnificence of your royal daughters. Only an untidy painter's studio, with a large easel quite visible and...and...

KING   Continue.

MARQUÉS   With Your Majesty's permission, I'll do so, for I know that the maestro's prudence inhibits him. The most intolerable feature of the painting is that it represents the glorification of Velázquez painted by Velázquez himself. He himself is in the painting, and Their Highnesses and all the others are on a visit to the studio of that conceited artist.

NARDI   I trust that Don Diego will ultimately agree not to paint it in such gross dimensions; for it would be, if Your Majesty will permit me a literary comparison, as if Don Pedro Calderón had written one of his great plays...in prose.

MARQUÉS   I don't have so much confidence in the judgment of a man who has perhaps dared, deep within, to consider himself in no way inferior even to Your Majesty's greatness.

KING   [*Angrily*]   What?

MARQUÉS   It seems that he himself has said that Their Majesties would be reflected in the mirror. He has not found even a tiny spot for Your Majesties in the painting, since he himself is depicted so large. It doesn't surprise me: I've never heard Velázquez pay any of the special tributes a vassal owes his monarch. And I doubt if Your Majesty has either.

[*The King thinks about this. The Infanta María Teresa enters through the curtain.*]

Her Royal Highness, sir.

[*The King stands. The Marqués and Nardi bow and move aside respectfully. The Infanta comes down the steps to her father and kisses his hand.*]

KING   And where are your attendants?

MARÍA TERESA   I preferred to come to you alone, sir.

KING   My daughter, can't you exercise better judgment?

MARÍA TERESA   May I remind you that you promised to allow me to attend the royal council? I yearn to discover what good judgment is, sir; that's exactly why I dared to ask you.

KING   Permit us to talk in private, gentlemen.

[*The Marqués and Nardi station themselves at some distance.*]

Today's sad business would have been too upsetting for a child like you.

MARÍA TERESA   You're mistaken, sir, if you think I'm too young to learn about sadnesses that I'll eventually know anyhow. In this palace they know everything: that we've lost the shipment of silver, that there's no money, that the country is hungry, that the war is not going well . . .

KING   Why should you think of those things? Your duties are praying and respectable pastimes suitable to your rank. Don't forget that!

MARÍA TERESA   Father, I only want to be of help to you. There are things that no one dares to tell you!

KING   [*Coldly*]   What things?

MARÍA TERESA   Do you know that three days ago no one ate in the palace except our family?

KING   What are you talking about?

MARÍA TERESA   And only yesterday, they couldn't serve the Queen a dessert she requested until one of the jesters offered a few coins, laughing, to pay for it.

[*A silence*]

KING   Marqués!

MARQUÉS   Sir . . .   [*He approaches the King.*]

KING   Why were there no sweets on the Queen's table yesterday?

MARQUÉS   Pardon, sir. It was the steward's negligence. He has already been punished.

KING   Is it true that there was nothing to eat in the palace three days ago?

MARQUÉS   We were speaking before of the vileness of the merchants, sir. But I would hold myself in low esteem if I had not taken the appropriate measures. The food supply is now assured.

KING   What measures?

MARQUÉS   Judicious measures, sir, against . . . the merchants.

[*The King bows his head.*]

KING   You may withdraw.   [*The Marqués bows and returns to Nardi's side.*]   Now you see that things aren't going so badly . . . Let your father deal with these difficulties as . . . he must . . .

MARÍA TERESA   Father, dare to choose other advisors!

KING   Don't try to show me how to choose the people who serve me! If you don't clear your head of these peculiar thoughts, it might be better for you to enter a religious order.

MARÍA TERESA   [*Standing straight*]   Sir, peace with France may depend on my marriage to King Louis.

KING   But maybe there will be no peace with France.

MARÍA TERESA   If God does not give you a son, I am the heir to your crown.

KING   [*Angry*]   That's what it's really about, isn't it? Are you already setting up your own court behind my back? It will be the convent for you if you incur my anger again!

MARÍA TERESA   Maybe I desire the convent more than you think. Maybe from there I could tell you with more authority to beware of bad servants . . . and pleasures that keep you from the business of state.

KING   [*Furious*]   Get out of my sight!

[*In tears, the Infanta genuflects and exits left. The King goes centerstage where he stands in thought. After a moment*]

Where were we supposed to go, Marqués?

MARQUÉS   To Velázquez's studio, sir.

KING   [*Feebly*]   Ah, yes. Velázquez. Then let us go.   [*But he doesn't move.*]

MARQUÉS   [*Softly*]   Usher . . .

[*The usher reappears and at a sign from the Marqués picks up the chair and exits.*]

When Your Majesty is ready.

KING   [*Looking in the direction of his daughter's exit*]   If I had a male child, another would carry on my line. The Queen is expecting again.

MARQUÉS   We would all celebrate that, sir.

KING   But perhaps there'll be another miscarriage...I've had the staff of Saint Dominic of Silos brought to the palace, and the sash of Saint John Ortega. They are said to be infallible in these cases.

MARQUÉS   Add to those venerated relics all the attentions that our lady the Queen fancies. I think, sir, it is the moment to construct the garden she asked of you in the Buen Retiro: nothing should annoy her now.

KING   It would be beautiful for her...five fountains, statues...But it will cost a hundred thousand ducats!

MARQUÉS   The money will arrive as the construction proceeds.

[*The curtains part to reveal Velázquez's studio.*]

KING   Yes, I owe her that happiness. Tomorrow I'll give the authorization. Let's see Velázquez now.   [*He reaches the steps and turns around.*]   Thank you, Nardi. You may leave us.

[*Nardi bows and exits right. In the studio, Velázquez stands motionless with his back to the easel and facing the audience. His hat, cloak, and sword are on the upstage table. The King goes up the steps, followed by the Marqués. Velázquez kneels. The Marqués stops near the first balcony window. The King goes close enough to Velázquez to permit the painter to kiss his hand.*]

Rise.

[*Velázquez stands up, watching the Marqués out of the corner of his eye. The King looks at the sketch. A silence*]

VELÁZQUEZ   May I proceed with the painting, sir?

KING   Wait for me outside, Marqués.

[*The Marqués exits with reverences upstage left, closing the door behind him. A pause. The King crosses as he speaks to sit in the armchair.*]

I find more pleasure in your paintings than any others. But that canvas is indeed strange. Do you believe that I understand something about painting?

VELÁZQUEZ   Your Majesty has seen fit to love and protect the arts as few
    other kings.

KING   With discernment?

VELÁZQUEZ   [*Thinking carefully*]   Your Majesty likes my painting. There
    are painters who detest it. Your Majesty understands more than
    they do.

KING   Sit beside me.

VELÁZQUEZ   With Your Majesty's leave.   [*He sits.*]

KING   If I had to explain to the Marqués the reason for my fondness for
    you, I could say scarcely more than this: my court painter intrigues
    me. It's been...how long have you been with me?

VELÁZQUEZ   Thirty-three years, sir.

KING   For all those years I've been waiting for a word of praise from you.
    They all tell me I'm the greatest monarch on earth. The painter says
    nothing.

VELÁZQUEZ   I'm not a man of beautiful words, and there are already
    many others eager to sing Your Majesty's praise. Why should I be
    only another voice in the chorus?

KING   We have grown old together, Don Diego. I have true affection for
    you. What meaning is hidden in that painting?

VELÁZQUEZ   It represents...one of the truths of the palace, sir.

KING   Which truth?

VELÁZQUEZ   I don't know how to say it...I believe that truth exists more
    in the simplest moments than in formality. Then everything can be
    loved...the dog, the dwarfs, the child...

KING   Are you referring to the Infanta Margarita?

VELÁZQUEZ   Yes, Majesty.

KING   Is that all she is for you?

VELÁZQUEZ   She is nothing less than a child. Her Highness is a lovely
    child.

KING   You always contradict me so tactfully.

VELÁZQUEZ No, Majesty. It is only that Your Majesty honors me by permitting a dialogue.

KING [*Severely*] You're contradicting me again.

VELÁZQUEZ Forgive me, sir. I thought that the dialogue was continuing.

KING What would you say if I granted you the Cross of Santiago?

[*Velázquez laughs.*]

Are you laughing? I was expecting a few words of gratitude from you at last.

VELÁZQUEZ I was thinking of some of the people who wear it.

KING At one time or another you have hinted that you would like to belong to a military order.

VELÁZQUEZ True, sir. Since genuine nobility is not always recognized... and for some a painter is no more than a servant...I do desire a cross for my breast.

KING Which one?

VELÁZQUEZ It could be the Order of Santiago, sir. [*He laughs again.*] And I'd consider myself very honored if the Marqués were my sponsor. [*The King stands and Velázquez follows suit. The King takes a few steps.*]

KING Have you ever been unfaithful to your wife?

VELÁZQUEZ [*Perplexed by the unexpected question*] I think...not, sir.

KING Don't women arouse you?

VELÁZQUEZ Women still attract me, sir. But...it seems to me too serious a matter to treat as a game.

KING Are you suggesting that women are a game for me? [*A silence*] Answer!

VELÁZQUEZ Heaven frees me from judging Your Majesty.

KING We're all made of clay. It is a sin, I know that, but... [*He looks at Velázquez with his gloomy eyes and goes to the sketch which he studies. Mumbling*] A sad life. A sad life.

VELÁZQUEZ May I undertake the painting, sir?

KING [*With a look of annoyance*] I still haven't decided.

[*He puts on his hat and strides upstage. Velázquez kneels. The King opens the door at left and exits. The Marqués is waiting on the landing and bows. They disappear. Immediately we hear the sound of a halberd striking the floor and a sentinel call: the King! Velázquez gets up, looking toward the door. A guard farther away repeats: the King! Velázquez suddenly picks up the sketch as if he intended to smash it angrily against the floor. A third call, very distant, by another guard is heard. At the same time, the door upstage right opens and Nieto enters.*]

NIETO   What's going on, cousin?

VELÁZQUEZ   What?...Nothing. I was trying to decide about a pose. [*He replaces the canvas gently on the easel. Nieto steps forward.*]

NIETO   When are you beginning the large painting?

VELÁZQUEZ   I don't know.

NIETO   Did His Majesty approve it?

VELÁZQUEZ   No.   [*He crosses to arrange some paint pots and brushes on the desk. Looking around with precaution, Nieto speaks confidentially.*]

NIETO   Be very careful, cousin. You have powerful enemies. I mustn't name them, but I know that they're plotting something against you.

VELÁZQUEZ   [*Pressing his arm affectionately*]   Thank you. I know who they are.

NIETO   Maybe you don't know the worst of them all...

VELÁZQUEZ   And who is that?

NIETO   I'm not referring to anyone of flesh and blood; rather to...the Enemy.

VELÁZQUEZ   The enemy? Oh, of course!   [*He smiles.*]   Always seeing evil spirits in the corners, my dear cousin.

NIETO   [*Very serious*]   I don't know if you are aware of his presence... he's listening to us now.

VELÁZQUEZ   [*Considering it a moment*]   But naturally the Lord protects us against him always. I doubt that I'm in any more danger than usual.

NIETO   You'll see. I find nothing censurable in that painting everyone is

talking about. But it does seem to me...how shall I say?...
indifferent.

VELÁZQUEZ [*He sits.*] Well! That's a very keen observation. What is
your idea of a painting that isn't indifferent?

NIETO One of saints, for example. You've painted some very lovely ones.

VELÁZQUEZ And I'll paint some more, no doubt.

NIETO [*Excited*] It gives me joy to hear you say that! As a painter you
must choose the correct path! If perchance you've been harboring
the thought of executing some irreverent painting of a mythological
subject that is excessively profane...

VELÁZQUEZ [*Laughing*] You forget that I could hardly paint an excessively profane mythological subject even if I wanted to. It's forbidden.

NIETO [*Looking at him hard*] To be sure: it is forbidden.

VELÁZQUEZ So there's no danger.

[*He catches sight of Pareja who has appeared upstage left leading
Pedro. He goes quickly to meet them.*]

Thank you, Juan.

[*To Pedro*]

Come over here.

[*Pareja waves a farewell and exits, closing the door behind him.
Velázquez leads Pedro downstage.*]

Are you tired?

PEDRO A little.

VELÁZQUEZ Sit down. [*He helps him sit in the armchair. To Nieto*] He'll
make a good model. He has a fine head.

NIETO I'll leave you.

VELÁZQUEZ [*Coldly*] Don't disturb me. [*He crosses and looks for charcoal on the table.*]

NIETO I only wanted to warn you...for your own good. I trust you'll
give it some thought.

VELÁZQUEZ Of course. I shall have to learn to protect myself from all kinds of enemies.

NIETO [*He hesitates taking his leave.*] I don't think I ever saw this man...Is he perhaps the new jester they were going to bring?

VELÁZQUEZ [*Laughing*] Jester? I hardly know him...Ask him yourself.

NIETO [*Baffled, to Pedro*] Are you the palace's new entertainer?

PEDRO I'm afraid I'm not deformed enough for that.

[*Velázquez represses a smile.*]

NIETO [*Perplexed*] No, no he isn't...God keep you, cousin.

VELÁZQUEZ And He you, cousin.

[*Nieto exits left and closes the door. Velázquez puts down the charcoal at once.*]

We're alone now. Do you want to see my trial sketch?

PEDRO Show me. [*He gets up. With Velázquez's help he gets to the easel.*]

VELÁZQUEZ It's getting dark. I'll open another window.

PEDRO Don't...My eyes see better this way.

[*A long pause. Pedro is contemplating the sketch with great attention. On the left exterior balcony, half-hidden by the door frame, Doña Isabel sits down with her vihuela and begins to play the first Fantasia of Fuenllana. Doña Agustina, with a dreamy air, leans on the opposite side of the balcony. Pedro steps back to see better.*]

Poor animal...He's tired. He makes you think of a lion, but the Spanish lion is only a dog now.

VELÁZQUEZ [*Nodding in agreement*] The curious thing is, they've named the dog "Lion."

PEDRO It's not curious: it's unfortunate. We come to accept the names. [*A pause*] Yes, I think I understand.

[*Velázquez gives a sigh of gratitude.*]

A calm painting; but with all of Spain's sadness within it. Whoever sees these beings will understand how hopelessly condemned to sorrow they are. They're living ghosts of people whose truth is death. Whoever looks at them tomorrow will do so with awe. Yes, with awe, for there will come a moment, as is happening to me right now, when he'll wonder whether he is the ghost in the presence of these figures...And he will want to save himself with them, to embark on the motionless ship of this room, because they are looking at him, because he is already in the painting when they look at him. And, perhaps, while he seeks his own face in the mirror, he is saved for a moment from dying.

[*He rubs his eyes with his hands.*]

Forgive me...I should have spoken to you of the colors, like a painter, but I can't. I can hardly see. I probably said some stupid things about your painting. I've come too late to appreciate it.

VELÁZQUEZ   [*Who has listened, profoundly moved*]   No, Pedro. This painting was waiting for you. Your eyes transform the sketch into the larger canvas...just as I shall try to paint it. A painting of poor beings saved by light...I have come to suspect that the very form of God, if He has form, must be light...It cures me of all the insanity of the world. Suddenly I see...and I'm filled with peace.

PEDRO   What do you see?

VELÁZQUEZ   Anything: a corner, the shaded tints of a human profile... and a terrible emotion possesses me, and at the same time absolute calm. Then it passes...and I can't understand how I've been able to enjoy such beauty in the midst of so much pain.

PEDRO   Because you are a painter.

VELÁZQUEZ   Why haven't you painted, Pedro? Your failing eyesight senses the painting better than mine. You fill me with humility.

[*The music stops. The two Meninas converse silently.*]

PEDRO   I'm tired. I can't see...   [*As Velázquez leads him to the chair*]   I went to Salamanca as a servant to a noble student. His father paid for my studies and I served him...Whenever I could, I went to the studio of Maestro Espinosa. He wasn't famous...Have you heard of him?

VELÁZQUEZ   No.

PEDRO   My parents were poor farmers...After three years of study, Maestro Espinosa managed to convince them to put me with him as an apprentice. When it was about to be settled, my master stole a

hundred ducats from another student as a prank. They searched
our quarters and found the money on me.

VELÁZQUEZ   On you?

PEDRO   He had hidden it in my bags to save himself...They tortured
me. I couldn't accuse the son of the man who had helped me...I
could only deny it, and they didn't believe me. I was sent to the galleys for six years.

VELÁZQUEZ   Dear God...

PEDRO   The sea is very beautiful, Don Diego: but an oar is not a brush.
When they freed me, I had little desire left to paint and I had to earn
my keep as best I could. I went back to my village. I suffered there
for eleven years. Even my parents believed I was a thief. When the
war broke out in Flanders, I enlisted. I told myself: I'll become
another man there. But war, close up...   [*He makes a sound of
revulsion.*]   Are you sure no one is overhearing us?

VELÁZQUEZ   Yes.   [*The two Meninas exit from the balcony, still carrying on
their unheard conversation.*]

PEDRO   I thought I heard a noise.

VELÁZQUEZ   [*Sitting beside him*]   Go on.

PEDRO   Why? I've lived as best I could. I had no time to paint.

VELÁZQUEZ   I feel I owe you something...

PEDRO   Someone had to paint what you have painted, and you have done
it better than I would have.

VELÁZQUEZ   If your reward has been a lifetime of pain...I can find no
satisfaction in my work.

PEDRO   Who ever told you you should find satisfaction? You've also
painted from your pain, even in the palace. Painting is your privi-
lege...don't belittle it. Only the person who sees the beauty of the
world can understand how intolerable its pain is.

VELÁZQUEZ   Then...do you absolve me?

PEDRO   [*Smiling*]   You are greater than I am, Don Diego.   [*Suddenly he
bends over, his face contracts.*]

VELÁZQUEZ   Are you ill?   [*He gets up and runs to the desk to fill a cup.
Pedro groans. Velázquez returns to his side and gives him a drink.*]   I'll

call a doctor to see you. You'll lack for nothing as long as I live.

PEDRO   Are you going to shelter someone who earned his degree in the galleys?

VELÁZQUEZ   [*Replacing the cup on the desk*]   That account is long settled.

PEDRO   Don't decide so quickly.

[*Velázquez turns around and looks at him.*]

But...are you sure no one is listening?

VELÁZQUEZ   You can't hear a thing through those doors. I'll check this one.   [*He opens the door at right and looks out. Then he closes it.*]   The other painters have gone.

PEDRO   Come close. I must tell you something...You were still a boy when it happened. In Flanders...in one of the Spanish regiments. Not in mine, no...in another. The country wasn't totally impoverished yet, and one could find food. But the soldiers were hungry. They'd had the misfortune to get a bad captain; his name was... Bah! I've forgotten the poor devil's name. He didn't give the soldiers their pay, and he was stealing from their provisions. If anyone complained, he'd have him beaten mercilessly. There was talk of going over his head to the general, but no one dared. Complaints usually have bad consequences...One day they whipped three men who took some food from the kitchen, and one of them died. Then the regiment's lieutenant challenged the captain and...killed him.

[*Velázquez steps back, shocked.*]

He killed him in an honest duel, Don Diego. He was a humble young man who had risen through his merits. A man without caution, who could not bear injustice...But he killed his superior, and he had to flee.   [*A pause*]   If he's still alive, I can guess what's probably become of him. In Lorca more than a thousand men have risen up against the unjust taxes. In La Rioja they killed two judges in February over the wine tax. In Galicia peasants burned all the official papers because their olive oil was taxed again. In Palencia they burned the harvest rather than hand it over...The whole country is dying of hunger, Don Diego. And, just as in Flanders, they answer with beatings and executions...No, I don't think that lieutenant has stayed far from those troubles, as long as his strength held out. But he must be a very old man by now...He's probably worn out, wishing to die peacefully like a dog in its kennel...If someone gave him shelter, he would be running a serious risk. [*A great silence. Velázquez looks him straight in the eyes.*]

VELÁZQUEZ   Let's go home.

[*Pedro is crying. Velázquez goes to him and lifts him up.*]

Rest on me.

[*They start upstage.*]

PEDRO   I'm old. Forgive me.

[*Velázquez gathers up his hat and cloak and opens the door. He exits with Pedro, leaving the door open so that he can continue to support him. A brief pause. The wooden shutters of the second balcony creak and open up. Nicolasillo appears from behind them. He looks around and comes out running. He stops a second before the easel and with a contemptuous grunt, he sticks his tongue out at the sketch. Then there are voices from offstage. It is the unintelligible conversation that the Marqués and Doña Marcela are having as they come down the steps toward the studio. Seeing the door open, they stop.*]

DOÑA MARCELA   Shhhh! It's open.

[*The Marqués steps forward and glances around from the doorway. Nicolasillo hides behind the easel.*]

MARQUÉS   There's no one here. Thank you for your confidence, Doña Marcela. Trust me.

[*They are about to leave. Nicolasillo steps forward.*]

NICOLASILLO   Excellency.

MARQUÉS   What are you doing here?

NICOLASILLO   I want to speak with Your Excellency. It's important.

[*As they stand looking at each other, the lights dim and the curtains close. The scene shifts to Velázquez's house. It is growing dark. Through the balcony at left, Doña Isabel is seen crossing with a lighted lamp. The interior remains illuminated. Juana enters by the door at right with a lamp which she leaves on the desk. She directs her words toward the open door.*]

JUANA   Set the table. Don Diego won't be long.   [*When she turns around she encounters Velázquez and Pedro who are entering through the curtains.*]

VELÁZQUEZ   Juana, I'm going to use this man as a model. He will live in our house.

JUANA   Here?

VELÁZQUEZ   Have the attic room prepared for him and give him a plate of food in the kitchen.

JUANA   The attic is used for storage. It's full.

VELÁZQUEZ   Then you'll have to make a space without delay.   [*They look at each other. Juana wants to refuse but doesn't manage to.*]

JUANA   [*Curtly*]   As you command.   [*She exits right, her face flushed.*]

PEDRO   [*Shaking his head*]   Don Diego, I've never had a wife, or children. That was not to be either. I couldn't forgive myself if I caused you to quarrel with your wife.

VELÁZQUEZ   There will be no quarrel, and my family will come to be yours. By God it will!

JUANA'S VOICE   You girls, go up to the attic. Take everything out and leave it in the hallway. We'll decide where to put it tomorrow. No need to scrub the floor. Set up the small cot. Put on the old sheets... That's all that's necessary. A candle? So that it can get knocked over and we all burn up? I should say not! Well, be quick about it.

[*Velázquez has listened with a hard expression. Juana reenters.*]

If you want to eat, there's a place for you in the kitchen.

PEDRO   God repay you for your kindness, señora.

JUANA   Thank my husband.

PEDRO   [*Juana starts to show him the way.*]   Don't bother, señora, I know the way.   [*He exits right. Velázquez sits down.*]

VELÁZQUEZ   I beg you to treat that man more civilly.

JUANA   Isn't that asking a lot?

VELÁZQUEZ   Tomorrow they'll scrub the attic room, and you will put a candle there for him. I also want you to give him some clothes. He's half naked.

JUANA   If it's no more than that . . .

VELÁZQUEZ   Sit here, Juana.

JUANA   I have things to do.   [*She starts to leave.*]

VELÁZQUEZ   Juana!

[*She stops, her chin quivering. He gets up and goes to her side.*]

You've always been compassionate. Aren't you going to take pity on an old man who has nowhere to go?

JUANA   He'll frighten the children . . .

VELÁZQUEZ   You're the one he frightens.

JUANA   He may be a thief. He could give us some sickness.

VELÁZQUEZ   His only sickness is his years.

JUANA   Think about it, Diego! How do we know he isn't the Enemy himself?

VELÁZQUEZ   Juana, I forbid you to talk with our cousin!

JUANA   You are bewitched, you're under a spell and you don't know it!

VELÁZQUEZ   Don't talk nonsense!

JUANA   [*Screaming*]   Send that man away!

VELÁZQUEZ   Don't scream at me! And listen: you have to learn to respect that man because . . . because . . . he is the person who matters most to me in the world today.

JUANA   [*Screaming*]   More than I?

VELÁZQUEZ   [*He presses his hands together violently.*]   In another way! I'll explain to you!

JUANA   [*Pointing; tearful*]   Your hands again!

VELÁZQUEZ   [*He separates them with a gesture that is almost threatening.*]   Enough!   [*He exits right.*]

JUANA   Diego, think of me! Send him away! I'm begging you because I care for you so much! . . .   [*Velázquez enters again.*]

VELÁZQUEZ   Where is he?

JUANA   In the kitchen.

VELÁZQUEZ He's not there. He must have heard you. He must have gone
out by the side door.   [*He starts to exit.*]

JUANA It's God's will, Diego!

[*Pedro comes out through the main door and takes a few hesitating
steps.*]

VELÁZQUEZ If I don't find him, Juana, I'll never forgive you.

JUANA Diego!

VELÁZQUEZ Never!   [*He exits right.*]

JUANA [*Taking the lamp and following him*]   Diego!

[*Pedro crosses downstage. His uncertain walk suggests how poorly
he sees.*]

PEDRO Martín.   [*He searches in vain.*]   Martín!   [*He stops, gasping for
breath. Doña Isabel and Doña Agustina meet in the window of the left
balcony.*]

ISABEL The Infanta has gone to sleep. Come out on the balcony.   [*They
step out.*]   They say that tonight we'll be able to see a ball of fire
over Madrid. A nun from San Plácido foresaw it in a dream.

AGUSTINA Yes?

ISABEL It will be a sure sign that our lady the Queen will have a male
child who'll rule in the world.   [*They look up at the sky.*]

AGUSTINA If only we could see it.

PEDRO Martín!. . .

ISABEL Who is that?

AGUSTINA It must be some drunkard. . .

[*They look up at the sky again. Velázquez comes out the main door
and looks in all directions. Slowly he approaches Pedro.*]

Look!

ISABEL Where?

AGUSTINA Isn't that it? Isn't that the ball of fire?

[*Doña Juana comes out the main door and holds up the lamp, trying to see her husband in the fading light.*]

ISABEL   Yes. I think I see it!. . .

VELÁZQUEZ   Come home, Pedro.

PEDRO   Let me go, Don Diego.

VELÁZQUEZ   No, I can't. Come. Give me your hand.

[*Pedro extends his hand timidly. Deeply moved, Velázquez takes it
tightly before the troubled eyes of his wife. They stand that way a
moment, while the entranced Meninas try to see something in the
sky.*]

CURTAIN OR FADEOUT

LAS MENINAS
Part Two

Original notation for Milan's First Pavan for the Vihuela

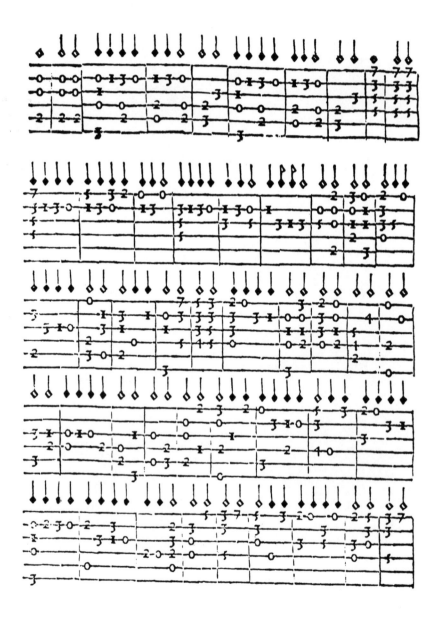

PART TWO

Before the lights come up, we hear the melody of Milán's "First Pavan." It is mid-afternoon. Centerstage represents the studio. The upstage door is ajar. Seated with her vihuela at the grilled window at left, Doña Isabel is playing for her own pleasure. Pedro and Martín are seated on the steps. Pedro is now wearing the clean and simple clothes of a servant. He has a far-away expression as he gazes out into the emptiness.

MARTÍN Do you hear her? She's like a canary in a cage. I don't envy them, no indeed. When they aren't playing, they're yawning. That's how it is in the palace. What are you thinking about?

PEDRO That painting. . . It can't be bought with all the light in the world.

MARTÍN [*Irritated*] I don't know how much nonsense I've heard from you about that painting! What do you know about it if you're blind as a mole?

PEDRO But I do see it.

MARTÍN They've curdled his brain for me in there, ladies and gentlemen. Stuffing your belly is the best way to lose your wits. Have you gotten over your fever?

PEDRO No, it still comes back. They bled me, but it didn't help. What about you? Are you getting by?

MARTÍN [*He shrugs and holds up the rope.*] I work at the same things I always did. Not much, though. They've raised the sales taxes again and nothing is going well. . . Do you remember that little ditty they used to recite in the old days? Well, they're saying it again.

PEDRO Which one was that?

MARTÍN A tax to sell, a tax to buy,
And soon we'll pay a tax to die.

[*They laugh. Doña Agustina appears at the grilled window.*]

AGUSTINA The little Infanta has awakened from her siesta!

ISABEL I'll go to her at once! [*The two women disappear.*]

PEDRO Do you want me to speak to Don Diego for you?

MARTÍN Later on maybe. I can still manage. [*He gets up.*]

PEDRO Come back later. I'll have something for you. [*He gets up and the two men start toward the door of Velázquez's house. Juana appears on the balcony.*]

JUANA   Pablo!

PEDRO   Coming, señora.   [*Juana looks at him suspiciously and goes back in.*]

MARTÍN   They've got you well trained, haven't they?

PEDRO   She doesn't care for me. She's good. . . but a little foolish. I do care for her.

MARTÍN   As long as they give you a free meal, you can laugh at all her foolishness.

PEDRO   All her foolishness. . . Martín, I would have given anything to have a wife like her.

MARTÍN   [*With a gesture to his head*]   Crazy as a loon! Are you thinking of getting married at your age? You'd try the patience of a saint!

[*He exits right, grumbling. Pedro enters the house through the main door. A moment before, Nicolasilla has opened the door at right and entered the workroom stealthily. He is tiptoeing upstage when Mari Bárbola runs down the stairs and peers in.*]

MARI BÁRBOLA   Where are you hiding? The Infanta is calling for you.

NICOLASILLO   Shhh!   [*He signals Mari Bárbola to come to him.*]   The Marqués has sent the other painters away, and he's placed a guard at both doors: that one. . .   [*Pointing left*]   and that one.   [*Pointing upstage right*]

MARI BÁRBOLA   And what's so unusual about that? There's always a guard at that door.   [*Pointing upstage right*]

NICOLASILLO   But they never put one in the hallway before.

MARI BÁRBOLA   Then there must be new orders.

NICOLASILLO   You could only be a German! If there are new guards, it's obvious that there are new orders!. . . Something is going to happen. . . to Don Diego. Maybe they'll arrest him.

MARI BÁRBOLA   [*After a moment*]   You know something!

NICOLASILLO   Keep your voice down!

[*He turns around and motions toward the door where he entered. It opens and the King enters accompanied by the Dominican Friar.*]

KING   What are you doing here?   [*Silence.*]   Out! And don't come back today.

NICOLASILLO   Ah!...

KING   What does that mean?

NICOLASILLO   Ah!!...

[*The two dwarfs bow and leave on the run. They can be seen going up the stairs and disappearing. The King stands watching them.*]

KING   Last night I had a bad dream, Reverend Father.

[*A questioning look from the Friar.*]

Yes, I saw myself in a large room full of paintings and mirrors and...at the far end...there was Velázquez behind a table. He rang a bell and someone pushed me toward him...I was half naked, but I saw myself in the mirrors dressed in the royal robe and crown...When I got close to him, I saw that my court painter was very tall...He seemed a Goliath, and his enormous face was smiling at me...Finally, he raised his great hand and said: Nicolasillo and you must grow. I woke up in a sweat.   [*He smiles.*]   The wiles of Satan to disturb the serenity of my judgment!...Don't worry, Father. Your Holinesses have been very generous to put this case in my hands, and I shall examine it with the rigor our Holy Faith requires. All the more so, since Don Diego will have to answer today to another imputation no less grave. Yes! Perhaps his hour has come!   [*He and the Dominican turn upstage when they hear the Marqués's voice from the doorway.*]

MARQUÉS   Do you know the orders?

GUARD'S VOICE   Yes, Excellency.

MARQUÉS   Then repeat them.

GUARD'S VOICE   As Your Excellency disposes, no one will enter this door without express permission of Your Excellency, with the exception of Their Majesties and the painter Velázquez.

MARQUÉS   See that they're obeyed.   [*He enters and makes a reverence.*]   Everything is arranged, sir.

KING   You have placed guards at the doors?

MARQUÉS   I thought it the best way to assure the privacy Your Majesty
desired.

KING   It would seem that you put them there so that the word would
spread faster.

MARQUÉS   Your Majesty chose this room because he believed it the most
discreet place . . .

KING   But I said nothing about guards. It would have been enough simply to close the doors. The guard has already aroused suspicions.
[*He points right.*]   At this very moment people are strolling by or
looking into the courtyard. Doña Marcela de Ulloa and Don José
Nieto Velázquez, to name two.

MARQUÉS   If Your Majesty wishes, I'll withdraw the guard.

KING   [*Looking at him coldly*]   Let them stay. It would only make matters
worse.

MARQUÉS   Sir, Maestro Nardi is waiting in the next room in case Your
Majesty requires his presence . . .

KING   If it should prove necessary, you yourself will go to bring Her
Royal Highness here.

MARQUÉS   Yes, Majesty. May I know, sir, which is the principal accusation that has given occasion to this interrogation?

KING   Since you'll be present, you'll know in due course.

MARQUÉS   With the greatest respect, sir, I suggest that it should not be
limited to the principal accusation, nor to the other danger I respectfully indicated to Your Majesty. I foresee the necessity of a third and
very serious imputation.

KING   You've told me nothing about that . . .

MARQUÉS   [*With a gleam of triumph on his eyes*]   Because I still cannot say
it for certain, sir. I'm waiting for reports.

[*Velázquez appears upstage. The King notices him.*]

KING   Approach, Don Diego.

[*Velázquez bows and closes the door behind him. He walks up to
the King and kneels before him. The King lifts him up.*]

VELÁZQUEZ   Sir . . .

KING   I must speak to my court painter.

[*The Dominican and the Marqués bow and exit right, closing the door behind them.*]

Don Diego, I have been your friend more than your King. But very grave charges have been made to me against you, and now it is the King who speaks to you. Within half an hour you will appear here to answer them.   [*Softly*]   I shall be most pleased if you manage to disprove the accusations.

VELÁZQUEZ   I can respond now if Your Majesty wishes.

KING   Others are to be present.

VELÁZQUEZ   I'm beginning to understand, sir. Meanwhile, there are guards at the doors.

KING   What do you mean?

VELÁZQUEZ   I mean, sir, that these solemnities are beginning to seem more and more like a trial.

KING   It's only a private conversation.

VELÁZQUEZ   With witnesses.

KING   That's not the appropriate word.

VELÁZQUEZ   With my accusers?

KING   No, no . . .

VELÁZQUEZ   Well, then, with judges.

KING   I've told you it is not a trial! It's a . . .

VELÁZQUEZ   An interrogation, sir?

KING   You could call it that.   [*Pause*]

VELÁZQUEZ   Until today Your Majesty has sheltered me from the plotting of my enemies. Perhaps some ill-wisher has managed to take advantage of Your Majesty's good faith and . . .

KING   Do you think me a fool?   [*He moves to the chair and sits.*]

VELÁZQUEZ   [*Bowing his head*]   Forgive me, sir. Now I see that I have lost Your Majesty's trust.

KING   [*Lowering his voice*]   You never had it.

VELÁZQUEZ   Sir!

KING   No, because...I've never been able to understand you.   [*A silence*]   No one hears us except God, Don Diego. Ask your conscience. Do you have nothing to accuse yourself of?

VELÁZQUEZ   [*After a moment*]   I shall wait to hear the charges, sir. Must I remain here until then?

KING   [*With involuntary affection*]   Perhaps you can go to your house first...if you promise me to return in time. It is the friend who grants you this.   [*He suddenly becomes angry.*]   But no!   [*Standing*]   I still don't know if I should let you go! When I think that you pretended a purity that...that...

VELÁZQUEZ   Sir!

KING   Let me think.

[*He goes brusquely to the balcony as he speaks. He stands with his back to Velázquez but his inner conflict is evident. Velázquez tries to comprehend. The Infanta María Teresa has come out on the left balcony and calls to someone still inside. Mari Bárbola comes out.*]

MARÍA TERESA   I don't want them to hear me in there.

MARI BÁRBOLA   Nicolasillo told me about it. He thinks it's something against Don Diego. The Marqués can't hide his delight, and we all know he doesn't care for Don Diego at all. He's the one who placed the guards at the doors.

[*The Infanta looks into space, uncertain of her course of action. Mari Bárbola waits.*]

VELÁZQUEZ   I can think of nothing I've done to offend Your Majesty.

KING   Silence!

MARÍA TERESA   Go to the stairway...Keep me informed of everyone who enters and leaves. Hurry!

MARI BÁRBOLA   Yes, Highness.

[*She hurries off. The Infanta looks out again.*]

KING   [*Without turning around.*]   I grant you the half hour. Use it well.

VELÁZQUEZ Will Your Majesty not give me the slightest clue to the accusation that is being made against me?

KING [*Turning around.*]   Go to your house.

[*The Infanta exits from the balcony. Velázquez bows to the King and steps back. At his second reverence, the King speaks without looking at him.*]

Would you dare to destroy any painting of yours, Don Diego?

VELÁZQUEZ [*Beginning to understand.*]   I could hardly do so if it were no longer in my possession, sir . . .

KING I meant if it were. But don't answer. Go to your house.

VELÁZQUEZ [*He has understood.*]   Thank you, sir! With Your Majesty's permission.

[*He bows again and steps back. The curtains close, and the scene changes to Velázquez's house. The Burgundian guard crosses downstage from right to left. Doña Juana enters right, followed by Mazo. She is carrying a tray with pitcher and glasses which she leaves on the side table.*]

JUANA Don't ask me again.

MAZO Yesterday you let me go up to see it.

JUANA I did wrong. That painting shouldn't be seen again by anybody.

MAZO But those of us who've already seen it . . .

JUANA Especially those.   [*She crosses left and peeks through the shutters.*]   It should face the wall until we're all dead and buried. It has to be.

[*Velázquez, wearing sword, hat, and cape, crosses downstage from left. His face is somber. He stops centerstage for a moment and looks toward his house. María Teresa appears behind the glass windows of the balcony and observes him with cautious but intense attention. Beside her, Mari Bárbola. Velázquez continues his cross and enters the house. The Infanta peers out farther to follow his movements. There is anguish in her eyes.*]

MARÍA TERESA Return to your post!

MARI BÁRBOLA Yes, Highness.

[*She exits. The Infanta steps back from the window. Juana turns to her son-in-law.*]

JUANA   Did you know that he has also shown it to that man?

MAZO   To Pablo?

JUANA   Something is wrong with my husband.

[*Pareja enters through the curtains.*]

PAREJA   Don Diego has returned, señora!

JUANA   At this hour?

[*Velázquez enters through the curtains. Juana runs to his side.*]

Are you ill? You look strange!

[*Pareja starts to exit.*]

VELÁZQUEZ   Don't go, Juan. Are the servants about?

JUANA   They're upstairs. Pablo is in the kitchen. What's wrong with you?

[*Velázquez serves himself a glass of water and drinks.*]

VELÁZQUEZ   [*To Pareja*]   I'll begin with you, Juan. Have you spoken with anyone about the canvas I painted upstairs?

PAREJA   I, sir?   [*Juana moves aside, uneasy.*]

VELÁZQUEZ   Try to remember: some careless word that might have slipped out . . .

PAREJA   Only with your son-in-law, sir.

VELÁZQUEZ   Swear it to me.

JUANA   Diego! Is it that important?

VELÁZQUEZ   Do you swear?

PAREJA   I swear by my eternal salvation, sir!

VELÁZQUEZ   [*To Mazo*]   And you haven't spoken to anyone either, my son?

MAZO   With no one . . . except those present here.

VELÁZQUEZ   I shouldn't have to ask you, Juana. But only you three know of that painting. One of you has talked.

JUANA   You also showed it to Pablo...

VELÁZQUEZ   You don't know what you're saying.

MAZO   With the greatest respect, Don Diego...You offend us by doubting us and not him.

VELÁZQUEZ   That is true. He will have to hear this too. Pablo!

JUANA   Diego, don't bring him here!

[*Velázquez exits right and we hear him call "Pablo" again. Juana sits in the armchair. Velázquez returns with Pedro.*]

VELÁZQUEZ   Pablo, have you spoken to anyone about the painting I showed you upstairs?

PEDRO   To no one but you.

VELÁZQUEZ   My wife would prefer that you swear to that.

JUANA   I didn't say that!

PEDRO   Doña Juana would not give credit to the oath of a poor man like me. But you know that I have not spoken.

VELÁZQUEZ   Indeed I do.   [*To the others.*]   I have little time and I must find out which of you is lying before I go back to the palace. Let me know who it was, to spare us all further embarrassment.   [*Silence*] No?   [*He goes to Juana's side.*]   The key has never been out of your sight, Juana?

JUANA   No.

VELÁZQUEZ   No one could have seen it? One of the servants? The grandchildren?

JUANA   [*With a thin thread of voice*]   No one.

[*A pause*]

VELÁZQUEZ   Why did you despise me so much in Italy, Juan?

PAREJA   What are you saying, sir?

VELÁZQUEZ   I'm saying that you had begun to hate me at the end of our trip to Italy and I'm asking you why.

PAREJA   I've always loved you as the benefactor you've been to me.

VELÁZQUEZ Not always. You're lying. Then it could have been you. [*Angrily*] Was it you?

PAREJA I've sworn it wasn't, my master!

[*Velázquez goes to his side as the others watch anxiously. Juana gets up from the chair.*]

VELÁZQUEZ You had a generous master, but he was a master. And you hated him.

PAREJA No, no!

VELÁZQUEZ And perhaps you've made me pay now for your resentment. Now that I've freed you, you stab me in the back!

PAREJA [*Falling on his knees before him and trying to kiss his hands*] Forgive me, sir. I have lied, and I should never have done so!... [*Stifled exclamations from the others underscore his words.*]

VELÁZQUEZ Then confess!

PAREJA It's true that I resented you...But I haven't betrayed you. By the living Christ I haven't!

VELÁZQUEZ Why did you hate me? [*He shakes him roughly.*] Tell me!

PAREJA Because of...that girl in Rome.

VELÁZQUEZ What girl?

PAREJA The one you used as a model...She was...everything beautiful I had ever imagined in my life. I would have given anything for her...And if she had commanded me to put a knife in you, then...yes, I would have. But she laughed at me. She was a whore and she considered me beneath her. She called me a black monster...while she was giving you all her favors.

VELÁZQUEZ What are you saying?

PAREJA She found you much to her liking. Very much. She told me so herself...You were the greatest of painters. I was an apprentice. You were free and handsome. I was ugly and a slave...I was dying for her, and you...you...

VELÁZQUEZ I, what?

PAREJA You had her without lifting a finger.

JUANA Diego!

VELÁZQUEZ [*To Pareja*]   You believed that?

PAREJA [*In an outburst of supreme sincerity*]   And I still believe it!...
[*He slumps down in sobs. A short silence*]

VELÁZQUEZ And now you've had your revenge.

PAREJA No! It wasn't me. I'd die for you. My master! My master!...

VELÁZQUEZ Get up. Come, get up!   [*Pareja stands up and moves aside, overcome by his grief.*]

PEDRO Slavery is a terrible thing.

MAZO Why can't this man keep his opinions to himself?

VELÁZQUEZ This man can say anything he pleases, because it wasn't he. Can you say the same?

MAZO You offend me!

JUANA What has happened, Diego?

[*A pause*]

VELÁZQUEZ I've been denounced to the Inquisition.

JUANA What?

MAZO Because of that painting?

VELÁZQUEZ Because of that painting.

JUANA What can they do to you?

VELÁZQUEZ I'll soon know. My trial is this afternoon.

JUANA [*Wringing her hands*]   This afternoon?

VELÁZQUEZ Whoever has betrayed me, say so. I know that it was my fault. We should never confide in anyone. Juan, if it was you, I forgive you. Or you, Bautista. Maybe you did it without thinking, from the urge to talk about something astonishing...

MAZO Although your suspicions pain me, I won't attempt to dispel them. But I too suspect what you stubbornly refuse to admit...   [*He points to Pedro.*]   But there's no time left to set things straight. I can only try to help you, and I beg you to accept my humble assistance. It is the least I can do for the person I owe most.

VELÁZQUEZ How?

MAZO   Let me say that I was the one who painted that canvas.

[*Velázquez's expression suddenly changes.*]

VELÁZQUEZ   As proof that it wasn't you or from remorse because it was?

MAZO   Think what you like but accept my offer.

[*Juana sits down again. She is extremely distressed.*]

VELÁZQUEZ   I'm thinking something else...I believe they call you my rival and they flatter you by saying your painting looks like mine.

MAZO   I have tried to learn from you.

VELÁZQUEZ   [*Raising his voice*]   And you've also boasted around the halls of the palace that you had nothing else to learn from me.   [*Mazo looks down.*]   There are no secrets in the palace, my son. But you have yet to learn enough to do a painting like that! No, Bautista! Even if you did take the responsibility for me, you would never paint like that, even if you wished it with all your soul!

MAZO   Maestro!

VELÁZQUEZ   [*Contemptuously*]   Silence!   [*Looking at all of them*]   It's hard to be part of the human race, Pablo. Almost everyone is a slave of something.

PEDRO   Yes, every man...and woman.

[*Without warning, Juana breaks into tears. Velázquez looks at her and suddenly understands. He goes to her side. She looks into his eyes, and her sobs increase.*]

VELÁZQUEZ   [*To the men*]   Go outside.

[*Mazo and Pareja exit through the curtains.*]

PEDRO   It'll be better for me in the kitchen, Don Diego.   [*He exits right.*]

VELÁZQUEZ   So it was you.

JUANA   I can't believe that he has denounced you.

VELÁZQUEZ   He?...   [*He strikes his forehead with his palm.*]   Why I must be a fool. Our cousin José, obviously.

JUANA   He couldn't have said anything. He owes you so much...

VELÁZQUEZ   Reason enough. Did you show him the painting?

JUANA   [*In a whisper*]   Yes. But I did it to help you, Diego!

VELÁZQUEZ   Are you sure?

JUANA   Do you have any doubt?

VELÁZQUEZ   [*Looking at her fixedly*]   You're the one who has a doubt. You don't know if you've disobeyed your husband to help him or to do him harm.

JUANA   I. . . you?

VELÁZQUEZ   An intolerable doubt, isn't it? As you were showing him the painting, you kept repeating to yourself: I'm helping my Diego, I'm helping him. You wanted to see if you could silence another voice that was telling you: Hurt him a little. . . Not too much. But let him suffer. He made you suffer. He betrayed you with that woman. . . and others.

JUANA   [*Covering her ears*]   Be quiet! Be quiet!

VELÁZQUEZ   I don't blame you, Juana. You've reached the age of doubting. I should have foreseen it.

JUANA   You're cruel. . . You forget how little you've helped me. . . You humiliated me by shutting the door when you were with that prostitute; you've been humiliating me ever since Italy. . . You only think of your painting, ignoring a woman who is suffering the pain of growing old. . . and who has been faithful to you.

VELÁZQUEZ   Have you ever thought that you could be to blame?

JUANA   I?

VELÁZQUEZ   When we had been married for four years and were like two happy children. . . I asked you something that you refused. I never asked you again.

JUANA   What are you talking about?

VELÁZQUEZ   I asked you to be my model for a Venus I wanted to paint. And you refused. . . shocked, embarrassed, at odds with me for the first time. . .

JUANA   [*Her face betrays the sudden memory.*]   A decent woman could not do such a thing. My own father said so, and he was a painter.

VELÁZQUEZ   [*Contemptuously*]   He was a bad painter.

JUANA   No Spanish painter has done a painting like that!

VELÁZQUEZ   I have! It shouldn't surprise you that I had to look for other models when you refused. If you had agreed I would have painted you when you were still young, and now you would be happy, at peace, without doubts.

JUANA   [*After a moment*]   And that made you stop loving me?

VELÁZQUEZ   [*He goes over to her and caresses her hair.*]   I didn't stop loving you, Juana. I loved you so much...that it was impossible for me to betray you with another woman...here or in Italy. But I had to resign myself to the fact that you didn't understand. I feel no resentment. You've been my unselfish companion, in spite of everything. But I can no longer trust you.   [*He steps away. She gets up and runs to his side.*]

JUANA   Yes, you can! Give me another chance and you'll see.   [*A pause*]

VELÁZQUEZ   Very well.   [*Lowering his voice*]   In Italy I painted two other of those dangerous she-devils.

JUANA   It's always Italy!...

VELÁZQUEZ   They are in two palaces in Madrid. No one knows it except their owners. You won't be telling that to cousin José.

JUANA   No, no!...

VELÁZQUEZ   Now you see...that I do still love you.

JUANA   Diego.   [*She attempts a timid embrace which he tolerates.*]

VELÁZQUEZ   Give me the key.

JUANA   [*Hastily taking the key from her key ring*]   Yes, yes! Destroy it and I'll burn it! You can say it doesn't exist anymore, that it was only a study...

VELÁZQUEZ   [*He takes the key.*]   That painting will not be destroyed as long as I can prevent it! I'm taking the key so that you won't do it yourself.

JUANA   [*Completely shattered*]   What's going to happen to you?

VELÁZQUEZ   We never know what the punishment will be...a reprimand or the heretic's hood.   [*Furiously he strikes a fist against the palm of his other hand.*]

JUANA   [*Timidly*]   Diego, I am with you. . .

[*He turns around slowly to look at her with a smile of supreme self-confidence that is his exasperating strength. For a moment he looks at her in silence. His expression is absolutely serene.*]

VELÁZQUEZ   Don't worry. I'm not afraid.

JUANA   But you are!. . .

VELÁZQUEZ   No, because I see something. And it's marvelous.

JUANA   What?

VELÁZQUEZ   Don't move.

JUANA   [*She realizes that it is The Painter who is looking at her now and she screams.*]   Ah! I don't understand you! I never will!

[*She exits sobbing through the curtains. Pedro appears from right.*]

VELÁZQUEZ   [*With a laugh*]   Pedro, is the world really so horrible?

[*Pedro does not reply. Velázquez's expression darkens.*]

Forgive me. Looking at you I know that it is. I was afraid for you in the palace. I thought for a moment that they had discovered you. Then I understood that the King was talking about my painting. [*He goes closer to him.*]   I'm going to try something new, Pedro. I'll ask to meet face to face with my accusers. If I succeed, I may win the game. If not. . . we may not see each other again.

PEDRO   Take these words of mine with you, as if they were the last I would ever say to you.   [*He clasps his hand.*]   Since you are going to face lies and falsehoods, you must lie if necessary for the sake of your work, which is true. Keep your dignity, but be shrewd too.

VELÁZQUEZ   Thank you.   [*He exits rapidly through the curtains.*]

PEDRO   Good luck. . .

[*He lifts his shoulders in resignation. A pause. Juana returns. She controls her feelings with difficulty and manages a smile. Velázquez appears through the street door, followed by Mazo and Pareja. They cross, but before exiting left, Velázquez stops a second and looks toward his house. At that moment, Pedro takes one hand in the other in a gesture of grief.*]

VELÁZQUEZ   Let's go.

JUANA   If he cares for you so much, then so do I, Pablo. Tell him that... when he returns. I beg you.

PEDRO   I'll do my best, señora...Believe me.

JUANA   I'll bring you some bread...a half-loaf. I know that you share your food with another poor man.

[*She exits. Martín enters downstage right and sits on the steps. He scratches himself, yawns, and searches his leather pouch in vain. Juana returns with a half-loaf of bread.*]

JUANA   Here.

PEDRO   Thank you, señora. I'll go out for a while. You probably want to be alone.

JUANA   Yes. Come and go as you please.

PEDRO   With your permission, señora.

[*He bows and exits through the curtains. Doña Juana sinks down suddenly to her knees and crosses herself. The curtains close before her. From left a court official and two constables enter. Martín is frightened but decides not to move.*]

FIRST CONSTABLE   Do you think it's this one?

SECOND CONSTABLE   I know him. He's an old vagrant who hangs around the pedlars' stands.

OFFICIAL   The one we want doesn't have a beard.

[*They start toward the entrance to Velázquez's house and Pedro appears in the doorway. They stop and look at him. A signal of agreement crosses between them. Martín has stood up and has kept his eye on them. The constables approach Pedro from both sides, and the official cuts off his escape.*]

PEDRO   [*Trying to make out what they are doing*]   Huh? What?

OFFICIAL   Are you the man called Pedro Briones?

PEDRO   I don't know what you're talking about.   [*He tries to go on his way, but the two constables take him by the arms.*]

OFFICIAL   Pedro Briones, I arrest you in the name of the King.

[*Curious, Doña Agustina appears on the balcony and signals inside. Doña Isabel joins her shortly. Pedro struggles and drops the bread. The two constables seize him.*]

PEDRO   Let me go!

SECOND CONSTABLE   Just keep calm.

OFFICIAL   Don't resist! Come along quietly.   [*He starts left, followed by the constables who are dragging Pedro along with some difficulty. When they reach centerstage, Pedro manages to pull free and steps back, gasping for breath.*]

PEDRO   No, no!   [*He escapes right. The first constable quickly unsheathes his sword and runs after him, followed by the second constable.*]

OFFICIAL   Catch him, you fools!

FIRST CONSTABLE'S VOICE   Halt!

OFFICIAL   [*Exiting in pursuit*]   In the name of the King!

SECOND CONSTABLE'S VOICE   Stop!   [*The voices fade away in the distance. Martín picks up the bread that Pedro dropped and continues watching, aghast.*]

ISABEL   Who are they running after?

AGUSTINA   I don't know. He came out of the Treasury House.

[*To Martín, who is shaking*]

Hsss! Hsss!

[*Martín looks up at them.*]

Who was it?

MARTÍN   I don't know anything . . .

[*Still another "halt" is heard from very far-off. Uncertain what to do, Martín exits right, still watching the pursuit.*]

ISABEL   Probably some thief.

AGUSTINA   Madrid is infested with criminals. Let's go back inside.

[*They leave the balcony. The light on the façades dims as it comes up on the central area. The curtains slowly part to reveal the studio. The easel and its canvas have been pushed back against the*

*wall; all the doors are closed. In the foreground, a large chair with
smaller chairs at either side. The impression is not quite that of a
tribunal: the three chairs are not placed exactly in a straight line.
The King is seated in the center; at his left the Dominican, and at
his right, the Marqués. Having removed his street accessories,
Velázquez enters downstage right, approaches the King, and
kneels.]*

KING   Rise, Don Diego.

[*Velázquez stands.*]

The Holy Office has received an accusation against you. In its great
charity and in consideration of your services to the crown, it has
placed the case in my hands so that I, in its name, may proceed in
the manner due our Holy Faith. You are here to speak before God
and with complete veracity. You are an old Christian, without
Moorish or Jewish blood, and since you still are not subject to official charges, you will not be required to speak under oath. But do
not forget that you are appearing before your King when you
respond to our questions. And now, tell us: is it true that you have
painted in your quarters a painting of a woman lying on her side
without clothing or any veil to cover her flesh?

VELÁZQUEZ   It is true, sir.

KING   Are you familiar with the rule that the Holy Tribunal has dictated
against such paintings?

VELÁZQUEZ   Yes, Majesty.

KING   Repeat it.

VELÁZQUEZ   Whoever makes and exhibits lascivious images will be punished by excommunication, exile, and a fine of five hundred ducats.

KING   Do you consider yourself guilty?

VELÁZQUEZ   No, Majesty.

KING   Justify yourself.

VELÁZQUEZ   With Your Majesty's permission, I would like to clarify first
certain circumstances of the case.

KING   Speak.

VELÁZQUEZ   An accusation to the Holy Tribunal cannot give occasion to an examination unless, before or after, one of its members should act to produce evidence that confirms the suspicions. And, to my knowledge, I have not been visited.

KING   Suppose that you have been.

VELÁZQUEZ   Then, since the charity of the Holy Tribunal permits this private hearing, I beg Your Majesty to have the member of the Holy Office who has accused me appear.

[*The King and the Dominican speak in whispers.*]

KING   That cannot be granted.

VELÁZQUEZ   Sir: can the attendance of any person that I name for my defense be granted me?

KING   [*After a look from the Dominican*]   It is granted.

VELÁZQUEZ   Will that person be obligated to respond to any question I ask him?

[*An exchange of perplexed looks among the three examiners*]

KING   In our desire to favor your justification it is granted.

VELÁZQUEZ   I request that the Queen's Chamberlain and my cousin, Don José Nieto Velázquez, appear before Your Majesty.

[*Surprised, the King looks at the Dominican, who, head bowed, does not move. A pause underscores the royal hesitation.*]

KING   Marqués, bring Don José Nieto here.

[*The Marqués gets up, bows, and exits right. Velázquez takes a breath of relief and gathers his strength. The King consults with the Dominican while Velázquez crosses left to face the door.*]

Does the painting to which we refer still exist, Don Diego?

VELÁZQUEZ   I would hardly be able to destroy it, sir, believing myself innocent of wrongdoing.

[*The Marqués returns, followed by Nieto. He closes the door and sits down again. Nieto kneels before the King.*]

KING   Rise, Nieto. Your cousin Don Diego has my permission to ask you a few questions. Answer him truthfully.

NIETO [*Bowing*]   So I shall, sir.

VELÁZQUEZ With Your Majesty's leave. Come here, cousin. And forgive me if any of my questions seem indiscreet.

NIETO [*Coming down the steps to face him*]   Speak.

VELÁZQUEZ How long have you been associated with the Holy Office?

NIETO [*Looking at the King*]   That question, sir . . .

KING Answer.

NIETO I've enjoyed that undeserved grace for nine days now.

VELÁZQUEZ My congratulations. [*A slight bow from Nieto*]   Now I begin to understand: you are new at your job. But you told us nothing about it . . . Does the Holy Tribunal request secrecy?

NIETO It recommends a prudent reserve.

VELÁZQUEZ Even with your closest relatives?

NIETO I made up my mind not to tell anyone. That way I could never fall into error.

VELÁZQUEZ A most prudent resolution. And now tell me, cousin: are you the one who has denounced me to the Holy Tribunal because of a painting my wife showed you?

NIETO [*Thinking a moment*]   I can't answer a question like that.

VELÁZQUEZ There's no need! It couldn't have been anyone but you, and you are not going to be so cowardly as to deny your act before your King. But my other questions will be more general. I beg you to enlighten me. A painter can always fall into error . . . what does he know of such delicate matters?

NIETO You know very well that the execution and exhibition of lascivious images is forbidden. If you had remembered it in time, you wouldn't have taken up your brush.

VELÁZQUEZ [*Sighing*]   I remembered it in time, cousin, and I did take up my brush.

MARQUÉS That can stand as a confession.

VELÁZQUEZ No, Excellency. The rule speaks of painting and exhibiting. [*To Nieto*]   I have not exhibited it.

NIETO If my opinion is worth anything, I shall not hide it. My opinion is that the first time a Spanish painter dares such an abomination, he sets a very dangerous precedent. And severe measures are in order. Nothing is painted without the intention of showing it. And, sooner or later, other people do see it...Execution is equivalent to exhibiting.

VELÁZQUEZ   Tell me, then. If a scandalous painting is exhibited by a different person from the one who painted it, would you punish him with equal severity?

NIETO   I, in good conscience, would do so.

VELÁZQUEZ   I must be very stupid. After listening to you, I understand that rule even less.

NIETO   It is very clear and very simple.

VELÁZQUEZ   Not quite so clear and simple. Because you don't understand it well or you would have had to accuse His Majesty the King first.

MARQUÉS   [With a start]   What!

KING   [He places a hand on the Marqués's arm to impose silence and looks hard at Velázquez.]   What are you insinuating?

VELÁZQUEZ   Only that my cousin has been a victim of his own zeal and that he undoubtedly has not understood the prohibition of the Holy Tribunal. If he had, we would not see in several chambers of the palace certain Italian and Flemish paintings of mythological figures no more clothed than the one I painted.

[The King whispers to the Dominican.]

KING   I represent the Holy Tribunal here and I can show you that there is no inconsistency. The fact that those works of acknowledged merit were already painted and are hung in secluded places must have some consideration in the matter. Furthermore, their creators are not Spaniards, and we could hardly impose on them norms to which they are not subject.

VELÁZQUEZ   Then, sir, I ask the same consideration for myself. It is not right that we accept from my foreign colleagues what is punishable for Spaniards.

NIETO   No, Don Diego. The Spanish painter must set a higher example. And therefore the holy precept takes care that such a pernicious custom does not grow or prosper among our painters.

VELÁZQUEZ   Cousin, how would you describe a lascivious painting?

NIETO   One that through its theme or display of nudity can inspire lust and impurity.

VELÁZQUEZ   Would you prohibit all types of nudity in painting or sculpture?

NIETO   Without hesitation.

VELÁZQUEZ   Since I spoke of the palace before, now I have no choice but to mention the churches.

NIETO   [*Startled*]   What do you mean?

VELÁZQUEZ   Are you forgetting that the most magnificent figure in our holy religion is that of a nude man?

NIETO   [*To the King*]   Sir, don't permit him to make a mockery of our holiest objects!

VELÁZQUEZ   [*Shouting*]   I am not making a mockery of anything!   [*To the King*]   I am only saying what I said before, sir.   [*He points to his cousin.*]   His lack of prudence is evident. The churches had slipped his mind.   [*He turns his back on Nieto and moves away.*]

NIETO   Don't utter any more abominations!

VELÁZQUEZ   [*Turning around*]   We still have to determine if the person who sees abominations in others is not perhaps seeing what is hidden in his own heart.

NIETO   You're insulting me!

VELÁZQUEZ   I only want to remind you that clothing sometimes disturbs more than nudity . . . that clothing did not remove carnal temptation from the world.

NIETO   Even so! One should always avoid the most obvious causes for sin!

VELÁZQUEZ   Anything can be cause for sin, cousin. Even the holy images have been. And anything can edify us, even nudity, if we behold it with pure eyes.

NIETO   Our eyes are not pure. And even a child would tell you that some of his toys tempt him more than others.

VELÁZQUEZ   The same child would tell you that the toys that tempt him most are those that are forbidden.

NIETO [*With a malicious smile*] Are you going to keep on questioning a prohibition of the Holy Tribunal?

VELÁZQUEZ Don't try to frighten me with the Holy Tribunal. I trust that it will judge me more wisely than you. You have seen lewdness in my painting. But I ask you: where is that lewdness?

NIETO You answered that yourself: in the painting.

VELÁZQUEZ [*Going closer to him*] It is in your mind, José! Your eye is what sins and not my Venus! I have seen it pure; your eye besmirches it. My flesh is at peace; yours is in turmoil. Before suspecting that your cousin had fallen into the devil's clutches, you should have asked yourself if it was not you, and all your ilk, who are in his clutches and, thinking of him night and day, serve him all the better! You haven't married, cousin, but neither have you joined a religious order! You've chosen none of the roads for man's salvation. Why don't you dare to affirm before God that temptations of the flesh are your saddest secret?. . .Don't you have anything to say?

NIETO We are all sinners. . .we are sinners.

VELÁZQUEZ Don't take refuge in the plural, cousin. Speak for yourself. [*To the King*] Sir, I humbly respect the prudent rules that an inspired wisdom disposes, but I would dare to suggest another rule that is not against lascivious paintings but against lascivious minds that see obscenity in everything. [*He turns to the left. The King and the Dominican converse.*]

KING Why have you painted that canvas?

VELÁZQUEZ Because I am a painter, sir. A painter is an eye that sees Creation in all its glory. And before its glory is confirmed for us at the end of time, painting perceives it. . .The woman I have painted is very beautiful, sir, but the body of the crucified Lord that I painted years ago is beautiful too, and the nuns of San Plácido adore it every day.

[*The King and the Friar speak to each other. A pause*]

KING Do you have any other questions to put to Don José Nieto?

VELÁZQUEZ Yes, Majesty.

KING Do so.

VELÁZQUEZ   Cousin, I know that you are sincerely religious. Denouncing someone who carries your blood and to whom you owe your post in the palace must have been hard for you.

NIETO   You know, cousin, that I expressed my fears to you in private days ago. . .   [*He sighs.*]   But you did not give me the slightest indication of repentance. . .

VELÁZQUEZ   Since I know that you have done it after wrestling with your conscience, I shall ask only one question more.

NIETO   I beg Your Majesty to give me his permission to withdraw. . . This is very painful for me.

KING   As soon as you answer.

VELÁZQUEZ   Thank you, sir. Cousin: when I was named Chamberlain to His Majesty, you said in my house that His Excellency, here present, had recommended you.   [*He moves closer to him.*]

NIETO   That is true.

VELÁZQUEZ   I invoke your scrupulous conscience? Don't forget that, if you lie, God will hold you accountable! Would you swear before him that you were not thinking of obtaining my post when you denounced me?

NIETO   I am not obliged to swear. . .

VELÁZQUEZ   No one is obliging you. I'm asking if you would dare! [*Pause*]   No?

NIETO   [*In a husky voice*]   I swear it before God.   [*Regretting it immediately*]   Oh!. . .   [*He takes a few steps back, covering his face with his hands.*]

VELÁZQUEZ   Thank you, cousin.   [*To the King*]   I humbly beg the Holy Tribunal, when judging me, to keep in mind the errors of judgment of a member of the Holy Office who was excessively impatient to show his merits; one who is perhaps not yet free of personal ambitions and perhaps, perhaps. . . a perjurer.

[*A pause*]

MARQUÉS   Do you mean that in spite of having disobeyed a precept of the Holy Office your respect for its authority and that of the throne was always correct?

VELÁZQUEZ   Your Excellency has expressed it perfectly.

MARQUÉS   An examination of your paintings might suggest good reason to doubt it.

VELÁZQUEZ   Is Your Excellency the one who intends to judge my paintings?

MARQUÉS   I beg Your Majesty to permit Maestro Angelo Nardi to testify.

VELÁZQUEZ   Can it be possible? Your Excellency is making my task easier!

MARQUÉS   Don't be so sure of that.

KING   Bring him in.

[*The Marqués exits right. Velázquez returns to stage left.*]

NIETO   I beg Your Majesty to grant me leave to withdraw.

KING   Not yet. Stand over there.

[*He points behind him. Nieto, head down, goes to stand near the side table. The Marqués returns, followed by Nardi whom he instructs to go down the steps. Nardi kneels before the King. The Marqués returns to his chair.*]

NARDI   Sir.

KING   Rise.   [*Nardi stands.*]

MARQUÉS   Maestro Nardi, excellent painter that you are, you have been called to the presence of His Majesty so that you may give your opinion of the paintings of Don Diego Velázquez without allowing any consideration of friendship or courtesy to affect your appraisal. Would you say that Velázquez has been carrying out his duties as court painter properly?

NARDI   Sir: I wish to make it clear to my admired colleague that my poor opinions do not attempt to put in doubt either the recognized excellence of his talents or the good faith with which he has painted his works . . .

VELÁZQUEZ   You touch me, maestro.

NARDI   But I must respond according to my conscience, since His Majesty commands it. I believe that the artist Velázquez, whose mastery is evident, is not, however, a good court painter.

MARQUÉS Why?

NARDI How shall I say it?. . . In his work he has not, I think, maintained the proper proportions.

MARQUÉS What do you mean by that?

NARDI He has painted only one canvas that deals with war, when our glorious battles have been and are so frequent. And even "The Surrender of Breda" is, I believe, too peaceful a painting; it seems more like a scene at court than an heroic military event.

MARQUÉS [*Smiling*] Continue.

NARDI Even more serious, I find that he invites us to laugh at a glorious soldier of our armies in another canvas of his. . .

[*Rapid knocks on the upstage door which are then repeated. They all turn to look.*]

KING Who would dare?. . .

MARQUÉS The guard has definite orders.

KING And they dare to knock like that?

[*More knocks on the door*]

MARQUÉS Perhaps it's some urgent news.

KING Go see.

[*The Marqués goes upstage and opens the door as the others wait in expectation. The Infanta María Teresa enters.*]

MARQUÉS [*Bowing*] Highness! [*Surprised, the King and the Dominican stand up. The Infanta steps forward with an open smile that does not quite conceal her inner turmoil. The Marqués closes the door.*]

MARÍA TERESA Accept my excuses, sir. I was confident that the guards' orders did not extend to me.

KING [*Looking at her fixedly*] What is this all about?

MARÍA TERESA I have asked you on occasion to let me attend your councils. . . If you would pardon my audacity. . .

KING I am not conducting a council meeting.

MARÍA TERESA That's why I dared to think I might attend.

KING   Do you know why we're here?

MARÍA TERESA   [*Hesitating*]   Whatever the reasons. . . I beg you to let me remain.   [*The Marqués comes downstage slowly.*]

KING   [*Curtly*]   You must have had to summon a great deal of courage to take this step.

MARÍA TERESA   Why, sir?

KING   [*Slowly*]   Because you came convinced that I would not grant your request.

MARÍA TERESA   [*Thinking she has failed, she bows.*]   Forgive my boldness. . .

KING   [*Exchanging a look with the Marqués*]   My reply is not the one you expected. Stay.

MARÍA TERESA   [*Surprised*]   I give you my thanks, sir.

KING   You may regret it. Do you still insist on staying?

MARÍA TERESA   [*Weakly*]   I insist, sir.

KING   Sit beside me.

MARÍA TERESA   With your leave.

[*The King sits again. María Teresa and the Dominican sit in turn. She casts a glance in Velázquez's direction and the King notices.*]

KING   Continue, Maestro Nardi. You were telling us that our soldiers had come to be a subject of mockery for Velázquez.

[*The Marqués stations himself close to the Dominican.*]

NARDI   In his lighthearted painting of the god Mars, sir, it is clear that the figure is intended to represent a soldier from Flanders. And when it is not mockery, we find in Don Diego's paintings disdain or indifference, but *not* respect. One could say that he admits no distances between Their Majesties. . . and the dogs and jesters that he paints. The same could be said of his religious paintings: they are few in number, and I don't believe that they inspire devotion. He seems only to seek human qualities in what is divine.

VELÁZQUEZ   Are you speaking as a painter or as a courtier, Maestro Nardi?

NARDI I speak as what we both are, Maestro Velázquez: as a court painter.

VELÁZQUEZ Perhaps you have not mentioned my most courtly paintings...

NARDI It was your duty to paint them, and who can say if it was to your taste. It is clear that you delight most in painting those things which by chance or some sad natural cause turn out to be the least courtly. I give as an example, the ugly, stupid clowns.

VELÁZQUEZ Those unfortunates have a soul like ours...or do you consider them less than human 'and merely insects?

NARDI I dare say that you would paint insects with equal satisfaction.

VELÁZQUEZ I would, yes! But not you! What would the court say?

[*The Friar smiles.*]

NARDI In my opinion, sir, Don Diego Velázquez believes himself a loyal servant and tries to be one. But his capricious nature...rules him. It is like his famous abbreviated style... [*He scornfully mimics a few careless brush strokes in the air.*] Almost all painters attribute it to his failing sight...which prevents him from perceiving details. But I suspect he does it from whim. By painting that way he reveals his disdain for the model...even if the model is a royal one. I speak as a painter, of course, although I am a courtier too.

VELÁZQUEZ Answer me one question, maestro, as a painter. When you look at the eyes of a head, how do you see the outline of that head?

NARDI [*After thinking*] Imprecise.

VELÁZQUEZ That is the reason for the abbreviated style that you consider a whim.

NARDI You need only to stop looking at the eyes and concentrate on the lines of the head to paint them.

VELÁZQUEZ That's your opinion. You believe that an artist must paint things. I paint sight.

NARDI [*Raising his eyebrows*] Sight?

VELÁZQUEZ [*Turning his back on Nardi*] Sir: I'll speak no more of intentions. As he grants that mine are correct, I am ready to admit that he is moved by his love for the throne and not by a dastardly desire to obtain my post as painter to Their Majesties. Since he speaks as a painter, I shall limit myself to the question of artistic competence. I know that his is great...

NARDI   You are very kind to say so.

VELÁZQUEZ   Not at all! His Majesty acts prudently in resorting to your knowledge, as he would act with equal prudence by not crediting that knowledge if it proved false.

NARDI   I do not profess to be the most learned of painters.

VELÁZQUEZ   Sir: believe me when I say that his knowledge has astounded me. Especially as revealed in his Saint Jerome.

[*The Friar listens very attentively.*]

NARDI   It is only a carefully painted canvas of a devout subject.

VELÁZQUEZ   It is also a canvas that proves your understanding of the laws of color.

NARDI   [*Smiling*]   Don't joke, Don Diego. Color has no laws...

VELÁZQUEZ   Don't try to hide from us what you have discovered, maestro.

KING   [*Intrigued*]   What are you referring to?

VELÁZQUEZ   I've noticed, sir, a faint greenish mist that surrounds the green robe of his Saint Jerome. The maestro knows something about colors that I don't, I must confess.

NARDI   You exaggerate. It's only a way of giving softness to the shadings...

VELÁZQUEZ   With a greenish mist around the robe?

NARDI   You yourself employ such pleasant effects...

VELÁZQUEZ   I?

NARDI   [*Laughing*]   Do I have to remind you of a certain greenish mist that surrounds the breeches in your painting of Don Juan of Austria?

VELÁZQUEZ   Did you paint your little greenish cloud because you had seen mine? What an honor for me!

NARDI   [*Annoyed*]   It is only a simple coincidence.

VELÁZQUEZ   Coincidence? You forget that the breeches in my painting are scarlet.

NARDI   And what does that have to do with it?

VELÁZQUEZ   I painted the greenish mist because I had observed that reddish tints create a greenish hue around them.

KING   Well! That is curious.

VELÁZQUEZ   It is something that occurs in our eyes, sir, and I still don't understand it well. Maestro Nardi apparently understands it better. . .I believed that green creates a reddish hue. . .and he paints it green. Not because he saw me do it, no! It's a simple coincidence. Maybe it won't be long before we see the shadings of his Saint Jerome turn red. Or the robe itself, but that would require more work. I recommend the former because it's simpler, maestro.

NARDI   [Eyes down]   I know nothing of the laws you profess to know. The color gradations of a painting only aspire to beauty.

VELÁZQUEZ   He knows nothing, sir. He says so himself. I still know very little about the great mysteries of light; he, nothing. Is this the man who can judge my painting?

[Nardi is confused and unable to speak.]

MARQUÉS   These arguments between colleagues have little to do with the real issue. Speaking as a painter, Maestro Nardi has failed to see a basic truth: the censurable nature of your painting.

VELÁZQUEZ   Excellency, I beg you not to speak in that way. It doesn't become you.

MARQUÉS   [Roaring]   And why not!

VELÁZQUEZ   It's too subtle for you.

[The Friar smiles. The Infanta smiles openly.]

MARQUÉS   Sir, do you need more proof than that remark of his abominable insolence?

MARÍA TERESA   I don't see anything insolent about it, Marqués. . .Don Diego was only jesting like all the clever people from Seville.

[They all look at her in surprise.]

Perhaps I shouldn't have spoken. Forgive me, sir.   [*She lowers her eyes.*]

KING   [*He gives her a stern look and turns to Nardi.*]   Do you have anything more to say, maestro?

NARDI   Only one thing, sir. Almost all the painters I know lament the special favor you give to Velázquez's judgment.

VELÁZQUEZ   We know that, maestro. They almost all take pains to affirm that His Majesty lacks artistic judgment.

KING   [*Dryly*]   Thank you, Nardi. Wait with Nieto.   [*He gestures over his shoulder. Humiliated, Nardi bows and goes up the steps to stand near Nieto. To the Marqués*]   Do you have something to ask Don Diego?

MARQUÉS   Yes, Majesty. The news I was waiting for has arrived.   [*With a glance at the Infanta*]   If Your Majesty wishes first to inquire about a certain matter . . .

KING   You speak first.

MARQUÉS   With Your Majesty's leave. Chamberlain Velázquez, choose your words carefully now.   [*He stops at a sign from the King to whom the Dominican has begun to speak in whispers. The others maintain a respectful silence.*]

KING   Wait, Marqués.   [*The King and the Dominican exchange their confidences. Then both stand, and the Infanta follows suit.*]   His Reverence is leaving us now, Marqués. Would you accompany him to the door?

MARQUÉS   [*Stepping forward quickly*]   Your Reverence is leaving? I urge him to hear what I am going to reveal . . .

[*The Friar interrupts him with a gesture and says something to him in a low voice. It is obvious that the Marqués is insisting and that the Friar is refusing as he reaffirms something. The Marqués shows his disappointment.*]

As Your Reverence wishes.

[*The Dominican bows before the King and the Infanta. The King returns the reverence, and the Infanta kisses the rosary. Then the Dominican starts upstage, accompanied by the Marqués. There are reverences from the others. As he passes by him, Nieto rushes to kiss his crucifix, but the Dominican gives him a cold look and, with a brusque gesture of displeasure, quickly withdraws his*]

*rosary. Shamefaced, Nieto returns to his place. The Marqués steps
ahead to open the upstage door for the Friar, who gives a quick
blessing and exits. The Marqués closes the door and returns to his
place beside the King. The dialogue has resumed during these visual actions.*]

VELÁZQUEZ Am I to understand, sir, that the decision of my case has
already been made?

KING His Holiness only attended to advise. I am the one who decides in
the name of the Holy Tribunal. And I haven't decided yet. Sit at my
right, my child.

[*The Infanta complies. The Marqués sits on the opposite side.*]

MARQUÉS With your leave, sir. Tell me, Don Diego, how you define disobedience?

VELÁZQUEZ The opposition to any authority through act or thought.

MARQUÉS Do you affirm that you are obedient to royal authority?

VELÁZQUEZ I do.

MARQUÉS Since you have doubts about my ability to deal with subtleties,
I'll limit myself to facts. Do you know a man named Pedro Briones?

VELÁZQUEZ [*A second of doubt*] No, Excellency.

MARQUÉS [*With a malicious smile*] Indeed you do...An old man who
served you as a model years ago.

VELÁZQUEZ [*On his guard*] I've had many models...I don't remember.

MARQUÉS You give him shelter in your house, and you don't know his
name?

VELÁZQUEZ Whom do you mean?

MARQUÉS An old man you have recently taken in.

VELÁZQUEZ To be sure...A sick old man who collapsed when he came
to my house begging...I'm keeping him there for a few days until
he gets his strength back...He did serve as my model some years
ago, yes...But I don't know who he is.

MARQUÉS [*To the King*] He is Pedro Briones, sir. A former galley prisoner who murdered his military superior in Flanders; the instigator
of the tax revolt in Rioja. He has cost the lives of several of Your
Majesty's loyal subjects.

KING What!... [*After a moment to Nieto and Nardi*] Wait outside, gentlemen.

[*They bow and exit right, closing the door behind them.*]

Did you know about these things, Don Diego?

VELÁZQUEZ No...I knew nothing about them all these years.

MARQUÉS Would you swear to that?

VELÁZQUEZ Is this a trial?

MARQUÉS Even if it isn't, you have asked another person to swear. Now you do the same.

VELÁZQUEZ This is not a trial, and I will not swear. Ask me what you will, and I shall answer in good conscience.

MARQUÉS Do you affirm that you are ignorant of what I have revealed?

VELÁZQUEZ I know it now.

MARQUÉS [*Laughing rudely*] Were you unaware of it when you gave him asylum?

[*Silence*]

Answer.

VELÁZQUEZ [*To the King*] Sir, I don't want to know what that man may have done. I only know that his life has been hard, that he is decent, and that he deserves mercy. He will die soon; he is very sick. I ask mercy for him, sir.

MARQUÉS A way of asking it for yourself, isn't it? Because you knew about his crimes when you took him in.

VELÁZQUEZ [*Coldly*] That, Marqués, will have to be proven.

MARQUÉS [*Angrily*] That man told you about his life in this very room! And then you gave him shelter. As you see, I am well informed.

VELÁZQUEZ Can Your Excellency prove it?

MARQUÉS Your tricks won't work with me. I'll not bring my spies here. Confess, Chamberlain. You have no choice.

[*Velázquez loses his composure. He is afraid.*]

KING [*In a low voice*] Who overheard them?

[*The Marqués leans over and whispers a name in his ear.*]

MARÍA TERESA   [*Having done her best to catch the name*]   Father, your pardon...

KING   [*Harshly*]   What do you want?

MARÍA TERESA   I heard the name he told you. There is no greater gossiper or liar in the palace.

KING   [*In a threatening voice*]   Are you trying to defend Velázquez?

MARÍA TERESA   Sir...like you, I seek justice...

KING   [*Looking at her sternly*]   You'll have your turn to talk.

VELÁZQUEZ   Sir, if they torture that man, it will kill him...

KING   Does that matter so much to you?

VELÁZQUEZ   He is very old. They may be able to obtain a false confession from him.

MARQUÉS   It's not necessary for him to confess, Don Diego. Your disloyalty is proven. Besides, that man is no longer capable of saying anything.

KING   Why not?

MARQUÉS   He tried to escape when they were taking him prisoner, and he fell over an embankment. It seems his sight was poor.

VELÁZQUEZ   [*In an outburst*]   What did you say?

MARQUÉS   He is dead.

VELÁZQUEZ   Dead?

MARQUÉS   Your Majesty will no doubt judge Velázquez according to Your Majesty's own high standards. I have said all I had to say.

KING   All the evidence is against you, Don Diego. Do you have anything to say in your defense?

[*Velázquez does not hear. Trembling, he stares into space. Finally, hesitatingly, he moves toward the steps.*]

Do you admit your errors?

[*Velázquez begins to cry.*]

What's that? You weeping?

MARQUÉS   That is his confession.

[*The Infanta gets up to go to Velázquez's side. Her hand reaches out timidly toward him without daring to touch him.*]

MARÍA TERESA   Don Diego?

[*The Marqués stands when the Infanta gets up. The King watches her somberly.*]

KING   [*To the Marqués*]   Leave us, please.

[*The Marqués bows and exits right.*]

MARÍA TERESA   Don Diego, you mustn't . . .

KING   [*Icily*]   In your voice there is a sentiment unsuited to your rank.

[*The Infanta reacts without turning around.*]

I wonder if you will show the same distress when your father dies.

[*The Infanta is slowly regaining her composure.*]

I wonder if there are not two guilty people in my presence.

MARÍA TERESA   [*Turning around angrily*]   What do you mean?

KING   [*Standing up*]   Why have you come here? What is he to you?

MARÍA TERESA   It is not proper to speak that way to an Infanta of Spain in the presence of others!

KING   [*Going to her side*]   Then you admit it!

MARÍA TERESA   I admit nothing!

KING   [*He moves away abruptly and walks down the steps to stand downstage left.*]   It's no use for you to deny it. I've been told how you slipped away from your attendants to see this man, of your visits to this room on days when the painter locked the door.

MARÍA TERESA   What awful thing are you insinuating?

KING   I speak the language of experience. Perhaps you were not totally aware of what you were doing . . . a silly girl who let herself be . . . charmed. [*To Velázquez*]   But what about you? [*Walking toward him*]   How did you dare put your impure servant's eyes on my daughter? You, the faithful husband, the man who resisted temptation! A defender of rebels, arrogant, disdainful of royal authority, a liar! It's all clear to me now. You did paint with an obscene purpose. You protected a criminal because you had contempt for the crown...and you dared to turn the heart and mind of a royal person.

VELÁZQUEZ   Sir, you are badly informed.

KING   Don't you contradict me! I know what I'm saying. It was enough for me to watch you together here to confirm it. You will pay for this, Don Diego.

MARÍA TERESA   Father...

KING   You shut up!

MARÍA TERESA   I will not, father. If you speak the language of experience, I am now a grown woman and I know what I'm saying. Today I've seen only shameless envy disguised as accusations against the man who suffers the misfortune of being the finest painter on earth and a decent man. If he does not defend himself, I shall do it for him, because I also understand yet another resentful accusation...and I know its source!

KING   The fervor of your words proves what you are trying to deny. I've heard enough.

MARÍA TERESA   If I told you the name of the one who made the accusation against us, would you listen then?

KING   You can't give me any name!

MARÍA TERESA   Wasn't it Doña Marcela de Ulloa?

KING   [Baffled]   What? Even if it were...

MARÍA TERESA   It was she. Bring her if you wish, father! If she spies on us, I also have ways of keeping an eye on her! She wouldn't dare to deny in my presence that she thinks of nothing but Don Diego... She runs after him...

KING   Daughter!

MARÍA TERESA   Oh, yes, father! That depository of honor of the ladies of the court would hand over her own honor to Don Diego without a moment's hesitation...if only he would say the word...which he has never been willing to do.

KING   [To Velázquez]   Is that true?

VELÁZQUEZ I don't know what Your Majesty is speaking of.

MARÍA TERESA You are asking him? Let me ask her! I'll force her to admit that she spread slander from jealousy, from resentment, from desperation...

KING She didn't lie when she reported your visits to this room.

MARÍA TERESA But she speaks of them in your own language, father... In the language of experience...the language of evil thoughts...of sin. [*A silence. The King is confused. She steps forward.*] Father, if you punish Velázquez, you will be committing the most terrible injustice. He has been more loyal to you than those who attack him! [*A pause*]

KING [*Somber, he crosses to Velázquez.*] I always held you in esteem, Don Diego. From this day on, I don't know if you deserve my friendship. I never managed to read your eyes, and now they still tell me nothing. Yet I would like to judge you as a friend more than as a King. It is up to you to help me understand all that has been said here in a different way. I no longer want to know what is behind your eyes. Your word is enough for me. Can a subject refuse to openly affirm his loyalty and his love to his sovereign? You've had mine...If you declare to me your repentance and recognize your submission to my person, I'll forget all the accusations.

MARÍA TERESA Weren't his tears enough? He wept for the injustice you did him.

VELÁZQUEZ I wept for the man who has died, Highness.

KING For that man?

VELÁZQUEZ He was my only true friend.

KING [*In a hard voice*] Ah, then, I was not? Is that all you have to say to me?

VELÁZQUEZ Something more, sir. I understand what Your Majesty is asking of me. A few words of fidelity cost nothing...Who knows what one's real thoughts are? If I say those words, I'll be able to paint what I ought to paint, and Your Majesty will hear the lie he wants to hear to remain at peace...

KING [*Angrily*] What are you saying?

VELÁZQUEZ It is a choice, sir. On one hand, another lie. A tempting lie. It can only bring me rewards. On the other hand, the truth. A dangerous truth that can no longer change anything. If Pedro Briones were alive, he would repeat what he told me before I came here: lie if it's necessary, for the sake of your work. But he is dead. What is caution worth in the face of that death? What can I give to be worthy of him, if he has given his life? I won't lie, even if I should. A dead man prevents me...I offer him my barren life... [*Vibrantly*] The truth, sir, of my profound, my incurable disobedience.

KING   I don't want to hear your words!

VELÁZQUEZ   I must say them! Pedro Briones opposed your authority; but who forced him to rebel? He killed because his captain was profiting from the hunger of his own soldiers. He stood up against the taxes because those taxes were ruining the country. Does power only know how to silence with blood the outcry against its own errors?

KING   [*Disturbed but trying to speak without emotion*]   I have loved my subjects. I've only sought the country's happiness.

VELÁZQUEZ   Perhaps.

KING   Measure your words.

VELÁZQUEZ   No more, sir. Hunger is spreading, the air is poisoned, and truth is so intolerable that it must be hidden like my Venus. But I must speak the truth. We are living by lies or by silences. I have lived by silences but I refuse to lie.

KING   It is one thing to accuse us of errors, but an attack on the everlasting foundations of power cannot be tolerated. You are destroying yourself, Don Diego.

VELÁZQUEZ   Everlasting! Sir, I doubt that anything is everlasting. Everything is born to die: men, institutions...and time carries it all away. It will also take away this age of sorrow. We are ghosts in the hands of time.

KING   [*Pained, he steps away.*]   I have loved you...Now I see that you did not feel love for me.

VELÁZQUEZ   Gratitude, yes, Majesty. Love...I wonder if a person who is feared can ask for love.

KING   [*Turning around, almost humbly*]   I know something about sorrow too...about sadness...

VELÁZQUEZ   Pedro is dead.

KING [*Taking a step toward him*] Thanks to me you have been able to paint.

VELÁZQUEZ He wanted to paint as a boy. I am ashamed of my painting. Punish me. [*A silence. The King is staring at Velázquez obsessively.*]

MARÍA TERESA He has chosen. Now you choose. And consider it well: It is a very great man who is looking at you. He has spoken to you as your own conscience should have done. Would you send your conscience into exile? You can choose to go on fathering children with prostitutes...

[*The King suddenly looks at her.*]

...and punish the man who dared to show you that it is possible to be faithful. You can continue to slumber amidst flatterers who grow rich while the country starves. You can be scandalized over a painting to hide the sins committed in the palace. You can punish Velázquez...and your own daughter...for the crime of speaking out, maybe for the first and only time, as true friends. Choose now between truth and lies!

KING [*Sadly*] He has known how to make you love him more than I have. That is the greatest offense of all.

MARÍA TERESA [*Exchanging a look of deep understanding with Velázquez*] Don't call it love, my father. In this court where love means empty flirtations and unbridled passion, it is a sentiment...without a name.

KING [*Looking at them both*] I should punish you both...I should send you to a convent and you into exile. If God had made me like my forebears, I would not hesitate. But I won't.

MARÍA TERESA Because you are better than you believe, father.

KING No. I should punish the others too, but I won't do that either. I am the most miserable man on earth. [*Tired, he turns around and walks up the steps. He stops near the door at right. Velázquez crosses toward him.*]

VELÁZQUEZ I did speak, sir! I did! Remember that!

KING Enough! [*He is about to open the door. With his hand on the knob, he turns to Velázquez.*] Would you destroy that Venus?

VELÁZQUEZ Never, sir.

KING   [*Not looking at him*]   You will never show it to anyone, nor will it
leave your house as long as you live.

[*Velázquez bows his head. The King jerks open the door.*]

Gentlemen!

[*He returns to his chair and leans against the back. The Marqués,
Nardi, and Nieto enter and bow. The King speaks without looking
at them.*]

I respect all that has been revealed here. We shall take cautious
measures. Meantime, it is my will that it be kept secret and that
your conduct with the painter Velázquez be the same as always. Is
that understood?

ALL THREE   Yes, Majesty.

[*With a brusque gesture, the King picks up his hat and places it on
his head as he walks quickly upstage. The Marqués hastens to
open the door and kneels as the King exits. The others do the same.
Velázquez and the Infanta go up the steps. From offstage, we hear,
each more distant, the three cries of the guards: "The King."*]

MARQUÉS   [*From upstage, without emotion*]   I have no choice but to be
your friend, Don Diego. I am at your command. Highness. . .   [*He
bows and exits, leaving the door open. Velázquez watches him leave
without the slightest reaction.*]

NARDI   [*Smiling*]   You surely noticed, Don Diego, that I tried to speak in
your favor in so far as possible. I beg you to come by tomorrow to
see my painting. I want to follow your advice about the shadings. . .
[*Crushed by Velázquez's silence*]   Highness. . .

[*He exits rapidly at right and closes the door behind him. Nieto
looks at his cousin. Then he bows to the Infanta and starts
upstage. As he is leaving, he walks up the three steps to the other
door and opens it. He turns back and looks at Velázquez for a second. Meanwhile, the lights come up on the downstage apron, and
Martín enters right chewing on the half-loaf of bread that Pedro
had dropped during his arrest. Tired and sad, he sits at right on the
steps and continues to eat.*]

VELÁZQUEZ   [*With cutting irony*]   I'll put you in my painting, cousin, just
as you are! It's exactly what I was looking for!   [*His laugh turns
instantly into a sob as Nieto exits and disappears.*]   I'll paint you. . .

[*He turns around, his face bathed in tears.*]   . . .if I ever paint again.

[*He presses his hands together desperately. As he speaks, the Infanta goes to the table and picks up the palette.*]

MARÍA TERESA   He said that you must paint. And so you must. Finish the painting, Don Diego. . .without me.   [*She comes closer.*]   I can't appear in it now. Here.

[*She unclenches his hands gently and gives him the palette. Veláz-quez kneels and kisses her hand.*]

VELÁZQUEZ   May God bless you!

MARÍA TERESA   Yes. . .May God bless us all. . .and keep me awake.

[*She withdraws her hand and exits quickly upstage. Velázquez stands up and looks at his palette. Then he grasps it firmly.*]

MARTÍN   The story is about to end. . .I'll tell it in towns and along the roads as if I knew it all. . .I'm alone and I'll go completely mad: that's always a solution.

[*The curtains close over Velázquez's motionless figure, and the light fades. We hear Fuenllana's "Fantasia" played offstage on the vihuela.*]

They'll laugh at my nonsense, and I'll pretend that I've seen the painting. Pedro told me some strange things about it that I don't understand, but I'll repeat them like a parrot.   [*He looks at the bread.*]   Pedro. . .

[*The curtains slowly part.*]

He said: it will be a painting that can't be redeemed with all the light in the world. . .A painting that will encompass all the sadness of Spain. If someone would paint me a poster for the fairs, I could make my living pretending that puppets talk. . .

[*The curtains are fully open. The light on the apron has faded, and Martín is now a shadow that speaks. In the studio, the actors stand motionless in the positions their characters occupy in the painting "Las Meninas" under the light of the open transom. Upstage left, Nieto is standing on the steps just as he was seen shortly before. The little Infanta stands in all her innocence. The dog dozes. The figures of the King and Queen are outlined faintly*]

*in the mirror. On Velázquez's breast, the Cross of Santiago. The
great canvas rests downstage on the easel.*]

Illustrious audience, that is Don Diego Ruiz, who doesn't look as
stupid as he really is! He says:

RUIZ AZCONA   There are some who complain, Doña Marcela...But our
blessed country is happy, believe me...just as we are in the palace.

MARTÍN   While Doña Marcela thinks:

DOÑA MARCELA   Nothing happened...I'm worried...When I look at
him now, I know that I've lost him forever.

MARTÍN   And the others...

NICOLASILLO   Wake up, Lion! Wake up!

MARTÍN   But like me the little fellow doesn't know what he's saying.

DOÑA ISABEL   They say a fountain is gushing precious stones in
Toledo...

DOÑA AGUSTINA   They've finally found the bars of gold in the buried fortress...

MARI BÁRBOLA   Nothing happened to him...God bless Don Diego and
keep him safe.

MARTÍN   That hypocrite in the background says nothing, but little Lynx
Eyes watches him and thinks...

NICOLASILLO   Señor Nieto is crying...

MARTÍN   The little Infanta is silent. She is still innocent of all this. That's
why Don Diego loves her so much...and because she is made of
light. And what about him? What can the painter be thinking, he
who knows it all?   [*A pause*]

VELÁZQUEZ   Pedro...Pedro...

[*The music grows louder. Martín eats his bread.*]

CURTAIN OR FADEOUT

The Set for Velázquez's Studio

The elevated playing area between the two façades of the set extends a bit over the "street," and is some 6½ meters wide. Slightly flared for scenic convenience, it may extend as much as 11 meters in depth, simulated perspectively according to the dimensions of the stage. Except for the absence of a ceiling, it reproduces faithfully the so-called "Prince's Room" that became a workroom for court painters after the death of Baltasar Carlos. The walls are 4.42 meters high. On the left side, we see five balconies with double-leaf shutters and transoms, but only a portion of the first of these is necessary. The shutters of the second balcony are open at some point but not the transom; the third and fourth are always closed; both shutters and transom of the last are open at times. On the panels separating the balconies, vague copies in black frames that Mazo made of paintings by Rubens and Jordaens: Heraclitus, Democritus, Saturn, Diana. Above these, other small canvases of animals and landscapes barely visible in the shadows. In the upstage wall, two parallel doors of approximately 2 meters in height which flank the great mirror in its black frame; the small doors of two cupboards on either side of the doors. A console table under the mirror, and above it the two well-known mediocre copies of "Pallas and Arachne" at right and "Apollo and Pan" at left. These measure 1.81 meters x 2.23 meters and are clearly visible when the balcony shutters are open to illuminate the poor colorations of the copier. The door upstage right opens into another dimly lighted room where the painters kept their supplies and which provided access to other rooms in the palace. The door at left opens onto a landing and six steps rising to a second landing where another door opens inward to the right and reveals a short pulled-back curtain.

The right wall, which Velázquez's painting does not show us, has no openings except at the downstage end where another panelled door, similar to those upstage, opens into a spacious room also used by the painters. A few more copies of Flemish works complete the decoration of the room. We also see several unframed canvases stacked against the wall, in keeping with the work done in the studio. Among them is an oversized one stretched on a frame with double cross supports. Downstage, next to the door, a small desk with water service and Estremoz cups of several colors: red, violet, brown. The silver sandbox with stand that we see in "Las Meninas" is beside it. Farther away, another larger desk with the brushes, palette, maulstick, paint tubes, and jars of the painter's profession. At the approximate distance of the second wall panel, a three-legged easel slightly more than 2 meters high, situated slightly to the right of centerstage and holding a medium-size canvas with its back to the audience. A chair and two folding seats with cushions along the walls. At the level of the far corner of the second balcony, whenever the action requires it, the setting is transformed to suggest a room in Velázquez's house, and then the door at right is assumed to provide access to the rest of the house. Two simple curtains running from opposite sides are sufficient. Another double curtain at the intersections of the room with the two façades remains open and serves to separate the three stage areas.